P9-CDZ-167

Primary Movement
in Sign Languages

Primary Movement in Sign Languages:

A Study of Six Languages

Donna Jo Napoli

Mark Mai

Nicholas Gaw

GALLAUDET UNIVERSITY PRESS / WASHINGTON, D. C.

KH

Gallaudet University Press
Washington, DC 20002
http://gupress.gallaudet.edu

Library of Congress Cataloging-in-Publication Data

Napoli, Donna Jo, 1948-Primary movement in sign languages : a study of six languages / Donna Jo Napoli, Mark Mai, Nicholas Gaw.
    p.   cm.
  Includes bibliographical references.
  ISBN-13: 978-1-56368-491-3 (hbk. :alk. paper)
  ISBN-10: 1-56368-491-8 (hbk. :alk. paper)
  1. Sign language. 2. Deaf—Means of communication. 3. Comparative linguistics.
I. Mai, Mark. II. Gaw, Nicholas. III. Title.
HV2474.N38 2011
419—dc22

                                      2011001091

7/15/15

CONTENTS

Foreword

We began our work as a comparative study across five sign languages: American Sign Language (ASL), British Sign Language (BSL), Italian Sign Language / *lingua italiana dei segni* (LIS), French Sign Language / *langue des signes française* (LSF), and Australian Sign Language (Auslan). Our initial question was whether it was possible to identify (even roughly) sign languages by their prosody, and, if so, our goal was to offer such identification as a new way to typologize sign languages.

Once we had settled on direction of movement as the one prosodic factor to track, we found that prosodic identification of sign languages did appear to be possible. The languages in our study clustered with respect to several characteristics along genetic lines, with BSL and Auslan contrasting with LSF, LIS, and ASL—a heartening finding.

Interestingly, however, we also found characteristics with respect to which BSL and LSF behaved as a group while Auslan, LIS, and ASL behaved as a contrasting group. We hypothesized that sign languages that are direct descendants of a mother sign language and that have remained in the geographical home of the mother language (origin-bound languages) contrast with sign languages that have evolved in a different geographical home from that of the mother language and in contact with the indigenous sign languages of the new home (diaspora languages). This hypothesis is quite different from what one might expect given research on the history of spoken languages; reasons unique to how sign languages are disseminated may help account for it.

We also found certain ways that sign languages for which the contact spoken language is English (that is, BSL, Auslan, and ASL) contrast with sign languages for which the contact spoken language is a Romance language (LIS and LSF). We connect this fact not to aspects of the grammar of the contact spoken languages but to the frequency and nature of gestures accompanying speech in those languages.

Finally, we isolated some characteristics that set apart individual languages from all the others, and we generated a list of characteristics to compare languages and to assess their degree of similarity with respect to direction of movement path.

At that point a reviewer suggested we test our hypotheses on other languages, particularly on new languages and on languages that had little to no contact with either of the two language families of our other five sign languages. But by that point we three scholars had scattered to the winds—with only one of us remaining in the field of linguistics. Nevertheless, working by email and with only intermittent face-to-face meetings, we did manage to test our hypotheses against a sixth sign language: Nicaraguan Sign Language/*idioma de señas de Nicaragua* (ISN). Many of our results were confirmed, whereas others could not be tested (given the degree of contact between ASL and ISN). It is our fondest hope that some new research team will now take up the flag and march onward, perhaps by looking at village sign languages in Africa or Asia or both.

Many helped us in this project, and we give a blanket thank you now to all, as well as the following specific thanks. Adam Schembri, Bencie Woll, and, especially, Rachel Sutton-Spence were generous with comments on an earlier draft. Karen Emmorey, Susan Goldin-Meadow, Brian Joseph, Gaurav Mathur, and David McNeill allowed us to bounce ideas off them and offered feedback. Rebecca Black and Myles Dakan helped with initial work on documenting the characteristics of curve paths in spring 2008. Dorothy Kunzig helped in Xeroxing the dictionaries, took the photos of our ASL model, and drew the arrows on those illustrations. Rosanna Kim served as our ASL model. Steve Wang advised us on which statistical tests to perform. We also thank anonymous reviewers, without whom this book would be much impoverished and the final chapter would not even exist.

1

INTRODUCTION

The past fifty years have witnessed a flowering of research on sign languages, largely on their phonology and morphology but in more recent years increasingly on their syntax and semantics. The first decade of this century also experienced rich comparative work across sign languages. For example, the Sign Language Typology Research Group at the University of Central Lancashire in Preston, United Kingdom, often in cooperation with the Max Planck Institute for Psycholinguistics in Leipzig, Germany, has been and is presently instrumental in multiple projects. These projects range from cataloging and describing endangered and little known sign languages in a browsable corpus to studies of specific topics, such as negative and interrogative constructions, possessive and existential constructions, numeral incorporation, and agreement systems. The Sign Language Typology Research Group has also organized international workshops in which researchers of sign typology can get together and discuss their results. Ulrike Zeshan (2004a, 2004b, 2006) has been at the forefront of much of this work, particularly on interrogatives and negatives.

Additionally, there has been considerable work on word order in particular sign languages, (from the seminal work of Fischer [1975] and the classic work of Volterra et al. [1984] to many of the articles in Brennan and Turner [1994] and the considerable work since), although several factors seem to stand in the way of a word-order typology for sign. Although sign languages vary in many ways syntactically (see Perniss, Pfau, and Steinbach 2007), typically they

1

make substantial use of classifier predicates. (We have read about only two exceptions. One is Adamorobe Sign Language, used in an Akan village in eastern Ghana, which lacks classifiers for motion and location [Nyst 2007]. The other is Indo-Pakistani Sign Language, which Zeshan [2000, 27] originally reported to have "no systematically arranged paradigm of classificatory handshapes" but Zeshan [2003] later reported to have limited use of whole entity classifiers.)

Once we enter the realm of classifier predicates, we undoubtedly find movement from one indexed position to another, with all characteristics of the signing—from handshape, to palm and fingertip orientation, to location, to movement, to nonmanuals—potentially being determined by setting up a framework in which each physical element in the signed message is analogous to some action or participant (active or passive, including locatum) in an event (see, among others, McDonnell 1996; Vermeerbergen 1996; Sutton-Spence and Woll 1999; Leeson 2001), and this includes nonpresent referents (Engberg-Pedersen 2004). Additionally, it appears that context plays an enormous role in word order in sign languages, as seen in spontaneous conversation (compared with elicited data)—a fact that makes firm statements about particular word orders difficult to maintain (among others, see discussion in Deuchar 1983; Johnston et al. 2007; Jantunen 2008). So we expect much in common syntactically across sign languages in such utterances, which we do indeed find (Johnston 1989; Woll 2003; Vermeerbergen 2006; Napoli and Sutton-Spence n.d.), with questions of comparative word order receding in importance. Nevertheless, the field is fertile, and we look with optimism at the search for typological characteristics both at the level of more specific constructions being examined in the studies alluded to in the previous paragraph and at the overarching level of word order.

Phonetic Typology

In this book we look for overarching characteristics for typologizing sign languages by studying another component of the grammar:

phonetics. It is often possible just from overhearing a snippet of spoken conversation to recognize that a language we ourselves do not speak belongs to some larger group, such as Chinese, Slavic, or Athabaskan, based solely on sound properties, whether phonetic or phonological. In fact, this common observation is not trivial; artificial intelligence has been using prosody analyzers for language recognition for years (Waibel 1988). Likewise, when we hear a nonnative speaker of English speak English, we can often guess at the larger group her or his mother tongue (L1) belongs to, just from phonetic and/or phonological properties carried over in the transfer from mother tongue to a second language (L2)—in this case English. Although influences from L1 on L2 are complex, there is general agreement that phonemic inventories, allophonic variations, phonotactic constraints, and prosody are all likely to be involved (Flege 1987; Rochet 1995; Boula de Mareüil, Marotta, and Adda-Decker 2004), sometimes to such an extent, particularly with respect to vowel quality and prosody, that intelligibility is threatened (Munro and Derwing 1995; Mayfield Tomokiyo and Waibel 2001; Burleson 2007).

With that in mind, we set out to see if we could typologize sign languages by phonetic characteristics, in particular by characteristics of the paths of primary movement. We chose to look at this particular component of the sign for several reasons.

Some scholars have argued that movement in sign is comparable to vowels in spoken language (Liddell and Johnson 1989; Perlmutter 1992). And some have argued that the distinction between full and reduced movement in sign is comparable to the distinction between strong and weak vowels in speech (Wilbur 1985). Additionally, in syllables that contain final holds, movement accounts for 55% of the duration and the final hold accounts for 45% (Wilbur and Nolan 1986), a finding that suggests movement may figure prominently in the perception of rhythm and stress (Wilbur 1990). Consistent with these findings, many have claimed that movement represents a visual analogue of sonority (Brentari 1990; Corina 1990b; Perlmutter 1992; Sandler 1993). Building on much of this work, Brentari (1998) offers the prosodic model of sign syllables, analyzing the sign as (1) two sets of features organized in a hierarchical feature geometry (where a feature geometry is independently motivated for sign languages—see Sandler 1986, 1987, 1989; Corina 1990a; Sandler and Lillo-Martin 2006); (2) inherent features (including handshape and location), which are comparable to consonants in speech; and (3) prosodic features (movement, both primary and secondary—a distinction we address in chapter 2 in the section "Primary Movement Only"), which she compares with vowels in speech. Regardless of whether one assumes the prosodic model, the recognition of movement as (somehow) vocalic and (somehow) relevant to prosody has shed light on phenomena in a variety of sign languages, including the appearance of something comparable to vowel harmony in the acquisition of BSL (Morgan 2006) and the accentual prosody (speed, intensity, and manner of movement) relevant to poetic form in LSF nursery rhymes (Blondel and Miller 2000, 2001).

All this led us to suspect we would find the movement parameter the most salient in a phonetic approach to a typology of sign languages. In support we note that the parameters of movement and location exert a stronger influence on the retrieval of signs during language perception or production than do the parameters of handshape or orientation (Corina and Hildebrandt 2002; Dye and Shih 2006). The movement parameter, however, is complex in a number of ways that were not accessible to us in our particular database (described in chapter 2). Still, the primary movement path was, for the most part, transparent; hence our choice. Since we are looking at movement paths in isolated citation forms of signs (rather than in conversations) and without regard to other parameters of the sign (rather than noting context), this is a purely phonetic study. It is arguable that our study is a comparison only of (part of the) syllable nuclei of signs.

The very narrowness of our study's focus increases its potential to be important for typological considerations. To see this, consider, for example, syntactic studies. In comparing studies of syntactic phenomena, one faces the difficulty of different (or, worse, inexplicit) criteria for identifying syntactic units, of myriad theoretical approaches that affect one's interpretation of the results, and so on (see Johnston et al. 2007 for a detailed discussion of such problems in comparing studies on word order in sign languages)—factors that impede attempts at corroboration of findings and at a true understanding of findings. Another possible hindrance in the search for syntactic typologies of sign languages is that syntactic characteristics of the contact spoken language (especially of its written form) can influence those of the sign language (Fischer 1975; van den Bogaerde and Mills 1994; De Lange et al. 2004; Milkovic, Bradaric-Joncic, and Wilbur 2007; Yau 2008; Wojda 2010), particularly in the type of laboratory context so common to elicitation tasks (Deuchar 1983; Coerts 1994; among many others). Our study, instead, explicitly outlines our method of data collection and analysis, so others may attempt to (dis)confirm our findings without having to enter into any interpretations of a theoretical nature. Further, by looking at the direction of movement along a path, there is little chance that properties of the contact spoken language can influence our findings (although, in fact, we will see that gestures of the contact spoken language may be relevant, where whether those gestures are one-handed, two-handed and asymmetrical, or two-handed and symmetrical is the important factor, not direction of movement along a path). One might say, then, that a phonetic study like ours has the chance to offer an ideal typology of sign languages; indeed, the corpus is remarkably clean.

The Languages in Our Study

In this work we offer the results of a study of five sign languages: American Sign Language (ASL), British Sign Language (BSL), Italian Sign Language / *lingua italiana dei segni* (LIS), French Sign Language / *langue des signes française* (LSF), and Australian Sign Language (Auslan). We chose these particular languages for several reasons. First was serendipity: At an international sign conference at Swarthmore College (outside of Philadelphia, Pennsylvania) in spring 2008, we observed a conversation in which people were comparing ASL and BSL and claiming that BSL was rich in movements going away from the signer whereas ASL was rich in movements going toward the signer. This piqued our interest, so we questioned other signers there about the general idea, and some went as far as to claim that from watching a conversation at a distance, even without catching any particular lexical items, they could distinguish certain sign languages from other sign languages. We then set about trying to gather information on multiple sign languages and quickly found that either the corpora were limited or our access to them was inhibited by our inability to read the spoken language of the country the sign language is used in. So we opted for sign languages with dictionaries written in languages we read.

We settled on these five languages both because we read English, French, and Italian and because they offered the possibility of looking for generalizations within and across language families, as we will now discuss. We then added a sixth language to test some of our resulting hypotheses on.

Clusterings of Languages: Genetic and Origin-Bound/ Diaspora

BSL and Auslan share a common ancestor; likewise ASL, LIS, and LSF share a common ancestor, although in all cases there are multiple ancestors (as we will discuss). Accordingly, our selection of these particular five sign languages allows the possibility of finding genetic clusterings—which, in fact, we did. BSL and Auslan turn out to have a variety of similar characteristics, whereas LSF, LIS, and ASL group together in differing from BSL and Auslan on those characteristics and in a similar way.

We also found, however, that BSL and LSF cluster together on a number of phenomena, in contrast to the other three languages.

This prompted us to reconsider the pertinent aspects of the languages' histories. Although BSL and Auslan share a common ancestor (McKee and Kennedy 2000), Auslan also has influences from Irish Sign Language (ISL) and ASL (Johnston and Schembri 2007). And although ASL, LIS, and LSF share a common ancestor (see Lane 1984 and Van Cleve and Crouch 1989 for a discussion of the first Deaf school in the United States in Hartford, Connecticut, where Laurent Clerc and Thomas Gallaudet used LSF in teaching; also see Radutzky 1993, 243, for a discussion of the first Deaf school in Italy in Rome, where Tommaso Silvestri used the methodical signs of Epée from LSF), ASL has also had strong influence from the sign languages used in the United States before LSF was introduced (Woodward 1978). This is particularly true of the sign languages used in Martha's Vineyard, Philadelphia, and New York (Tabak 2006). LIS, likewise, was influenced by the sign languages used in Italy before the introduction of LSF, particularly by the signs used in Rome, Naples, Milan, Turin, Parma, Genoa, Pisa, and Modena (Radutzky 1993).

Given that the languages that developed from the earlier languages without much interference from or contact with other sign languages (BSL and LSF) exhibit certain similarities, we might conclude that the particular similarities are representative of an unadulterated stage, so to speak. The languages that experienced significant contact with other sign languages (ASL, LIS, and Auslan) may, accordingly, show the types of variation that can happen from such contact, including creolization or borrowing. We therefore have adopted the terms "origin-bound" for BSL and LSF and "diaspora" for ASL, LIS, and Auslan.

From the way the languages cluster on various characteristics, we conclude that languages with a direct line of descent are distinct from languages with a line of descent affected by contact with another language (or languages); this may surprise (and perhaps disconcert) readers. Certainly, at least as far as historical linguists are concerned, including Lehmann (1962), Crowley (1992), and Joseph and Janda (2004), no such distinction is generally made. Rather, the two are the same except when the contact is so extreme that the genetic tree is rerooted.

Indeed, such rerooting might have occurred with respect to ASL. ASL emerged mainly from two sources: the variety of LSF Laurent Clerc brought to the United States (Lane 1984; Sacks 1989; Van Cleve and Crouch 1989) plus the sign already in use on Martha's Vineyard (which probably was not a variety of BSL; but see Groce 1985). Woodward (1976), using glottochronological procedures (as in Gudschinsky 1964), compares the lexicons of ASL and LSF and concludes that the degree of similarity (less than 60% of the lexicon) is lower than one would expect from a daughter given that the split was as recent as 1816, unless, in fact, that daughter has been creolized (see Woodward 1989).

To the contrary, Lupton and Salmons (1996) argue that ASL does not meet the usual definitions of a creole, pointing particularly to morphology they analyze as inflectional (and, thus, atypical of creoles). Although it is debatable whether ASL really has inflections (Liddell 2003) and further debatable what types of inflections creoles actually do allow (Patrick 1999), and although many still analyze ASL as a creole, Auslan is certainly not a creole (Woll 1991), and we know of no argument claiming that LIS is a creole.

So our finding that the sign daughters with a direct line of descent cluster together and in some ways are more conservative than the diaspora daughters may, in the worst case, turn out to be purely specific to the languages studied here. We doubt that, however. A distinction between daughters of an earlier language that were exposed to multiple other language groups through migration and daughters of that language that were not so exposed sometimes occurs in spoken language as well. Thus, in the Romance languages, the daughters of Proto-Romance that stayed on the Italic peninsula and its islands (the original home of Proto-Romance) have in many ways been more conservative than their sisters outside the Italic peninsula that had contact with other languages—the language(s) of Sardinia, among the most isolated, being perhaps the most conservative (Posner 1996; Marazzini 1999; Maiden, Smith, and Ledgeway 2010)—although we note that Romanian is also strongly conservative in many respects.

There is an additional reason not to be shocked at our division between origin-bound and diaspora languages—a very strong reason. All debates about the creole or hybrid status of ASL aside, and all debates about what happens in the history of spoken languages aside, we note that the histories of ASL, LIS, and Auslan differ from the histories of many spoken languages in a significant way. Consider ASL. In 1817 Laurent Clerc and Thomas Hopkins Gallaudet, a Frenchman and an American man, respectively, established the Connecticut Asylum for the Education and Instruction of Deaf and Dumb Persons (which later was renamed the American School for the Deaf; Lane 1984). The school opened with seven students, by the end of the year had thirty-three, and continued to grow steadily. Rather than an entire community of LSF users coming to the United States, these two men brought LSF to a group of students who had already been using a variety of sign languages and home sign. So the new users of LSF far outnumbered the old users. The ground was fertile for innovation. And this type of scenario is not unusual for new schools for the Deaf. So one should not a priori expect the history of languages in such a situation to proceed in the same manner as the history of languages when whole communities of speakers move from one place to another (see Woodward 2010). To the contrary, one might well expect differences in how the languages evolve. And, as we will show, the diaspora daughters we examine in this study do cluster together on a number of characteristics.

A final point is in order here. Throughout this discussion we have treated LSF and BSL as separate languages with no significant interaction. However, during the 1700s and early 1800s some British and Irish teachers of deaf children traveled to France for training in pedagogy methodology (Woll and Sutton-Spence 2004). It is possible that borrowing occurred from Old LSF into Old BSL via these teachers. Further, Old LSF had an influence on Old ISL (Matthews 1996; Leeson 2005), and ISL has interacted with BSL (Leeson 2005). In sum, it is possible that during the history of BSL there has been minimal borrowing both directly and indirectly from (Old) LSF. At this point the existence of such borrowing is speculative, so we proceed with the widely held position that the two languages are genetically unrelated and without contact significant enough to affect their grammars.

Import of This Work

As far as we know, very little has been published in the way of cross-linguistic studies of sign language phonetics. The present work, then, contributes to an area begging for more research; it asks questions that need to be asked, and it offers tentative answers.

This study is highly descriptive and uses tools from mathematics and statistics for analysis rather than relying solely on linguistic theory. The upshot is that the methodology and findings here are potentially useful for scholars working on a broad range of sign languages who may wish to draw on it for use from various theory stances.

The analytical methods employed are new to the field of linguistics. We constructed Venn diagrams showing the set relationships of movement directions of signs using the program VennMaster, which was developed for biological research to show analogous overlaps of classes of gene transcripts. Although this innovative approach to analysis gives results that are only as reliable as the data source used, it opens possibilities for further exploration with other corpora. Additionally, this approach allowed us to explore questions that otherwise would be very difficult to explore, and it uncovered unexpected patterns, leading to fairly radical—possibly controversial—interpretations, such as the finding that diaspora languages behave differently from origin-bound languages, and such as hypotheses about young sign languages versus mature ones.

With this book, then, we hope to open new discussions in both diachronic and synchronic approaches to the linguistic typology of sign languages.

Testing Our Results

Given the innovative analytical approach employed here and the fact that our results offer unexpected hypotheses particularly with regard to historical change, our study bears a heavy burden. We therefore chose to add a sixth language to the study, one that could help us test our hypotheses concerning young sign languages and whose genetic relationship to the other languages is unstudied (as far as we know): Nicaraguan Sign Language/*idioma de señas de Nicaragua* (ISN), used at a school for the Deaf in Managua, Nicaragua, and established in 1977.

2

GATHERING THE DATA

The raw data analyzed in later chapters are presented in appendices B through D. Other raw data that do not fit into our figures and tables but are alluded to in the analyses in the text are found in appendix A.

Given the existence and prevalence of classifier predicates, the phonetic shape and prosodic structure of a sentence in sign can be greatly affected by the particular event conveyed. Indeed, for just about any manual movement within the signing space, one can imagine a situation in which that movement might be appropriate. That fact suggested to us that certain parts of sign sentences might be similarly constrained with respect to phonetics across sign languages (moving from one indexical point to another, for example) and thus be of less interest in a comparative study. The phonetics of individual lexical items, on the other hand, should show maximal difference. Accordingly, we focused on movement paths of individual lexical items within the frozen, rather than productive, lexical inventory of these languages (McDonald 1983; Brennan 1990; Taub 2001; Russo 2004; and others, building on the distinction in Klima and Bellugi 1979 between linguistically conventionalized and visually transparent parameters for signs).

This is not to say that the frozen lexicon is in any way more important or more salient than the productive one with respect to the linguistic study of sign languages in general. To the contrary, the productive lexicon plays a predominant role in sign language discourse and is crucial to any discussion of sign language syntax. Our focus, however, is phonetic; it is strictly on movement—in particular, on those properties of the movement parameter that situational factors of the communication event do not constrain or influence.

Additionally, our databases (dictionaries) are inconsistent with respect to the inclusion of productive signs, some giving several, some giving almost none. Thus the goal of not letting these inconsistencies color our results was one more reason to limit our study to frozen signs.

Gathering Data and Lexicographical Considerations

We started by looking at online video dictionaries and quickly found that to classify all the characteristics of primary movement that we thought might be relevant, we had to record by hand a page's worth of information on each sign. This was tremendously time consuming, especially given that we had to watch any single video clip several times to make a complete catalog entry. Further, we found that watching a later video clip of a different sign made us recognize additional characteristics we needed to keep track of. So then we had to rewatch the earlier video clips and enrich the entries.

And, finally, on comparing our initial findings across researchers, we found reassuring consistency, with only a small amount of subjective judgment in making these catalog entries (unavoidable in that we are humans, not computers, doing the sorting). The small differences were few, and, crucially, none of these differences concerned the determination of the direction of a movement path, which is the important phonetic feature being compared in this study. Instead, the variable judgments had to do with two types of signs. One type involved what we call "hops" (or bounces) from one location to another; some of us wanted to catalog the hopping paths as involving straight segments and some as involving arc segments. In the end, we decided that the dynamics of bouncing is what makes the path take on a slight and elongated arc, rather than the arc being arbitrarily chosen. So we cataloged hop signs as consisting of straight segments. The other type of sign involved a wrist rotation from one point on the path to another, where the very rotation of the wrist creates a visual arc perforce (as we discuss in caveat 9 in this chapter's section on cataloging curve paths). Here again we decided to catalog the path as straight unless the arc appeared to be greater than the minimal necessary simply from the physiological wrist rotation. This second situation, of course, although rare, allows varied judgments. We concluded it would be advisable to have all entries in all five languages put into categories by all of us as quickly as possible (dividing up the work, not duplicating it), with one person then going over the final sortings painstakingly and double-checking with the other two when subjective judgments were involved. That way we could (at least theoretically) control for any inconsistencies.

Our hope is that consistency in our judgments across the languages will mean that any subjectivity (which, we stress, never involves path direction but, rather, is limited to wrist rotation signs) does not compromise comparative results. The decision to have one person check all the signs (with consultation when necessary), however, meant the project would take much longer, or we had to either severely limit the number of signs we would catalog and face the question of how to ensure randomness in selecting those signs or find a less time-consuming way of gathering and sorting the data.

We opted to find a less time-consuming way of gathering and sorting the data. We gathered our information from these printed dictionaries:

> The American Sign Language handshape dictionary (Tennant and Gluszak Brown 2002)
> Dizionario dei segni (Romeo 1991)
> La Langue des signes: dictionnaire bilingue LSF/français, 2 volumes (Moody et al. 1997/1998)
> Dictionary of British Sign Language/English (Brien 1992)
> Dictionary of Auslan: English to Auslan (Bernal and Wilson 2004)

GATHERING THE DATA

And, when we added in a sixth language to test our hypotheses against, we used this printed dictionary:

Diccionario del idioma de señas de Nicaragua (Gomez 1997).

We photocopied the entire dictionaries, cut out the signs, and then put them into piles according to characteristics of the primary movement. In this way our corpus was large and was gathered and sorted in less than two years, rather than several.

Phonetic studies usually draw on small corpora that are somewhat precise in having been chosen because of a set of restrictive characteristics. Our study, instead, has as unlimited a corpus as possible, within the confines that we set up, and the only restrictive characteristic was the presence of primary movement. In this way, the dictionary approach allowed us to be more ambitious than the norm. In the various chapters of this book, we analyze 1,289 signs of ASL, 1,501 of BSL, 968 of LIS, 1,441 of LSF, 1,880 of Auslan, and 714 of ISN.

One cost, of course, is that it is sometimes difficult to interpret movement information from a static representation. The dictionaries we used varied in the ways they conveyed this information, some using diagrammatics (arrows and the like) only, others using Stokoe notation, others using descriptions, and others using combinations of these methods. When we felt unsure, we turned to online dictionaries for consultation. However, sometimes for a given lexical item the printed dictionary sign was not the same sign as the one we found online. And many times the printed dictionary contained lexical items not included in online dictionaries. We list our concerns of this nature in the caveat section below. But we note that these concerns do not have to do with direction of movement, which is the one characteristic we analyzed in depth in this study.

Another issue involves the dictionaries we chose. All dictionaries, whether of sign languages or spoken languages, are inaccurate and incomplete documentations of languages, perforce. Yet some are better in this regard than others. So an important question is whether the dictionaries we chose gave us accurate and representative information. No information is given about whether they were created on a proper lexicographical basis. It could well be that some entries are related variants not listed as such (and we have been told this is true of the BSL dictionary). Further, there was no systematic documentation of phonetic variation in lexical signs. It is, therefore, unclear whether the dictionaries perhaps present data weighted toward a particular dialect and, thus, slant our results somehow. For example, some dialects of BSL have been influenced by ISL (and vice versa), yet we have no information on which dialects of BSL our dictionary presents. The Auslan dictionary, on the other hand, presents one regional variety: that used in the state of Victoria; however, it is not based on linguistic principles. Johnston and Schembri (1999) discuss issues that come up in the lexicography of sign languages, important issues that could seriously affect the corpus; thus, although we stand in awe of the exacting and comprehensive work that went into the dictionaries we drew on, we realize that they may have used very different lexicographical methods, have various inconsistencies, and present incomplete documentation.

It was suggested to us that we run our study using an additional ASL dictionary, an additional BSL dictionary, and so on, as a way of getting around shortcomings of the particular dictionaries we used, including the fact that they might be biased toward particular dialects and they might reflect idiosyncrasies of their authors with respect to data gathering and presentation. This would certainly be possible for ASL (there are many dictionaries, some superb, such as Costello 1994) and for LIS (see the outstanding work of Radutzky 2001), and it may soon be possible for Auslan (we understand that Trevor Johnston is working on an online comprehensive lexicographical database of Auslan) and for ISN (the Asociación Nacional de Sordos de Nicaragua is working on a more comprehensive dictionary right now, but lack of funding has stalled the project).

However, the first suggested goal of such an extension of our study would not, in fact, be served by that extension. Biases toward one dialect will, at best, be augmented by biases toward additional dialects. Think of it this way: how is a study of the phonetics of English as spoken in Atlanta, Georgia, and as spoken in Boston, Massachusetts, any more representative of the phonetics of North American English than a study of just Atlanta speech or just Boston speech? If we truly want to get a handle on the phonetics of ASL across all varieties, for example, we need to gather many signs from signers at locations all around the United States and Canada where schools for the Deaf or communities of Deaf people exist; that is, a study comparable in scope to the study of North American English done in Labov, Ash, and Boberg (2005), where telephone surveys were carried out on 762 speakers from, literally, all the urbanized areas of North America. The same holds for the other languages studied here. Simply adding a few more dictionaries will not do it.

On the other hand, we agree that such an extension of our study, simply by augmenting the database, might well help to wash out the effects of idiosyncrasies in the way authors of particular dictionaries collected and presented data. To this end, one might want to aggregate the data from every available dictionary of ASL, then from every available dictionary of BSL, and so on. Nevertheless, we have not done this, for it is a huge job. Ours is an initial study of a new way of approaching the typology of sign languages. It is like building Rome—it will not take just one day (or year, or decade). We present our methodology clearly so that if others deem it promising, they may join in the vast amount of research ahead.

William Labov started his study of American phonetics with analyses of limited databases (Martha's Vineyard speech, New York City speech, Philadelphia speech, and so on). We do the same, hoping to get a comparative phonetic study of sign languages started. We do not purport to be the definitive word on ASL as a whole, BSL as a whole, and so on, although we will talk about ASL, BSL, and so on for ease of exposition. Instead, our studies are only of the data in each of these dictionaries, period. But we note that each dictionary we use easily offers a large enough database that the statistical analyses we carry out can be considered valid. Indeed, the size of our corpora is huge in comparison with most phonetic studies on spoken languages.

This is a typological study and was not intended as a way of ferreting out genetic relationships. There is a good amount of controversy over whether comparing entire lexicons or comparing just 100 or 200 carefully selected lexical items is the better way to assess genetic relatedness among languages in general and among sign languages in particular (see Padden [2010] and Woodward [2010]). It turns out that our study ranks as most similar those languages that, in fact, we know are genetically related. However, it does this by comparing across the frozen lexicon as a whole, rather than by comparing words with similar meaning (i.e., potential cognates). Thus our study is not directly pertinent to the points of issue in that controversy, and it might well offer a new tool for determining genetic relatedness.

We should add a final note pertinent to the fact that our data are drawn from dictionaries. Whenever we mention a sign from LSF, LIS, or ISN, we give it in the French, Italian, or Spanish translation and then we offer an English translation. We do this for two reasons. First, our data come from dictionaries in which the signs are translated into the spoken contact language (that is, French for LSF, Italian for LIS, Spanish for ISN, and English for ASL, BSL, and Auslan). By giving the French, Italian, or Spanish translation, our readers can know what French, Italian, or Spanish word to look up if they want to consult the dictionaries themselves.

Second, many signers in many sign languages engage in mouthing to varying degrees, where by "mouthing" we mean mouth patterns that are in some way derived from or related to the contact spoken language (Boyes-Braem and Sutton-Spence 2001). Italian signers, for example, are claimed to engage in mouthing to a great extent, more so than American signers (Padden and Humphries 1988, 120), and it is well attested that BSL signers use mouthing quite regularly as part of certain signs (Sutton-Spence and Day 2001). Although we know of no systematic study of this common claim, it is consistent with our own observations (see Ajello, Mazzoni, and Nicolai 2001). So giving the contact spoken language translation may in fact be giving information about the sign itself.

Primary Movement Only

This study examines only signs that have primary movement, not signs for which the only movement is secondary or a handshape change. In fact, all our dictionaries had many signs not involving primary movement—sometimes as many as 20% of the signs in the dictionaries did not involve primary movement.

Although the division between secondary and primary movement is one that goes back to early work in sign phonology (Liddell and Johnson 1989) and has been used in phonological analysis in important ways by many (Sandler 1989; Perlmutter 1992; Brentari 1998), the actual distinction between primary and secondary movement is not uncontroversial and is far from simple. We adopt here the kinesiological approach to the distinction in Mai 2009. Mai views secondary movement as occurring in the most distal articulator such that the points in space that the wrist and elbow occupy are fixed. That does not preclude changes in orientation of the wrist (as in pronation and supination movements, twists, and rotations).

One way to think of it is to imagine a room that is shaped like the old traditional lightbulb. There is not enough room to take a step forward, backward, or sideways in it, but you can manage to turn around by spinning in place. You can also bend from the hips in various directions and flail your arms around. Those limitations give an idea of the analogous limitations in secondary movement. This metaphor for secondary movement does not isolate a physiologically united group (for example, the elbow is involved both in the wrist twist of the ASL sign TREE and in the lowering of the forearm in the ASL sign DAY—but we say the former has only secondary movement, whereas the latter has primary movement), and we are not comfortable with our definition.

For the purposes of this study of direction of movement paths, however, it was necessary to set these signs aside since they do not have a path (with endpoints that differ from one another) per se. Indeed, many works refer to primary movement as "path" movement, distinguished from secondary movement, which they call "internal" movement (Sandler and Lillo-Martin 2006).

Cataloging Data

Our initial sorting was into the three now classic piles: one-handed signs, two-handed signs in which one hand is an immobile base, and two-handed signs in which both hands move (building from the groundwork first laid out in Battison [1978]).

Within each pile we extracted all the signs that involved distinct arcs, circles, or loops (traveling circles) from all other types of movement paths for separate analysis, since the curve itself has its own internal direction (clockwise [CW] or counterclockwise [CCW]).

Cataloging Signs with Noncurve Paths and the Existence of a Goal

We categorized all noncurve movement paths by direction of movement, always defining the direction in accord with right-hand dominance, with the exceptions we list below. (In the definitions of path directions here, the "signer's plane" means the plane in which the signer stands, stretching out to the right and left of and above the signer.)

Away = away from the signer's plane
Back = back toward the signer's plane
Contral = toward the contralateral side (i.e., toward the left of the signer for a right-handed signer)
Down = down
Ipsil = toward the ipsilateral side (i.e., toward the right of the signer for a right-handed signer)
Rear = rear (i.e., moving toward a point behind the signer's plane)
Up = up

Many signs involve repeated movement. Depending on the dynamics of the movement, we classified them as repeated in a particular direction or as swing signs (such as **Contral-Ipsil**, meaning swinging from side to side, and **Up-Down**, meaning moving up and down). Note that all straight path two-handed signs in which the movement of the hands exhibits reflexive symmetry across a plane but, importantly, with additive inversion, are automatically analyzed as swing signs.

Let us elaborate. By "additive inversion," we mean signs for which if we designated the middle point along the movement path as zero and the endpoints as +1 and −1, the hands would be at additive inverse positions along their respective paths at all times. So if one hand was at +.5, the other would be at −.5, and they would pass each other at zero (see Napoli and Wu 2003 for discussion).

Additionally, when one hand moves on a straight path in one direction and the other moves in the other direction only once, we analyze this as a single phase of a swing movement (with inversion).

We describe movements in relative terms (away from signer, toward the contralateral side of signer, etc.) rather than absolute endpoints. This method tends to winnow out movement differences between signers that may be due to their individual postures or personal physical attributes. Relative directions allow us to focus on the physiological movement possibilities of the articulator and thus allow more valid comparisons across signers and across languages.

In figure 2.1 we can see the cardinal directions with respect to one-handed (1H) signs.

It quickly became clear to us that the most common single goal of movement for 1H signs is to a point of (near) contact with the signer (even though the absolute directions **Away** and **Down** may combine with other absolute directions to yield an overall greater number of signs going in the sum of the combined directions). We lumped all such signs into one group, calling the direction of movement **Ts** (toward signer) without regard to the starting point of movement.

GATHERING THE DATA

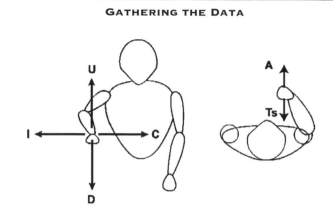

Figure 2.1. 1H Cardinal Directions
(U = **Up**; I = **Ipsil**; C = **Contral**; D = **Down**; A = **Away**;
Ts = Toward signer)

Conflating 1H signs with direction of **Ts** in this particular way ignores data about the starting point and thus reduces analytical and explanatory possibilities. Nevertheless, we believe this was the right decision, since this conflation allows us to capture the generalization that the goal of movement in 1H signs is the overwhelming converging factor when it comes to direction of movement, as our figures in chapter 3 will show. Including information on the starting point would have obscured this fact.

In figure 2.2 we see the cardinal directions, again, with respect to two-handed signs in which one is an immobile base (2HIB). Just as we saw with 1H signs, among 2HIB signs there is a single most common goal of movement: the base (which we defined as anywhere from the elbow down on the nondominant articulator). We lumped all such signs into one group, calling the direction of movement **Tb** (toward base) without regard to the starting point of movement.

Within 2HIB signs we noted two other movement prevalences. First, many signs involve movement of the dominant hand on, under, or near the base. We called such signs **OnB** (on the base), regardless of the direction of movement along that base (unless the movement was circular, in which case we cataloged it with curve path signs). Second, many signs involve movement of the

GATHERING THE DATA

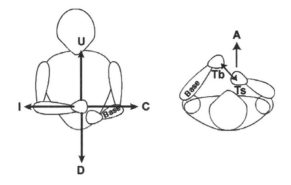

Figure 2.2. 2HIB Cardinal Directions
(U = **Up**; I = **Ipsil**; C = **Contral**; D = **Down**; A = **Away**;
Ts = Toward signer; **Tb** = Toward base)

dominant hand brushing past the base, typically making contact but not always. We called such signs **PastB** (past the base),
regardless of the direction of movement. We also maintained the
(nonabsolute) direction **Ts** for two-handed signs in which one was
immobile.

It is important to note that with 2HIB signs the movement direction we noted was always with respect to the nondominant hand.
So, for example, **Ts** indicates movement of the dominant hand from
the nondominant base toward the signer. And **Up** indicates movement from the nondominant hand upward.

Turning to two-handed signs in which both move, we find that
most move in a reflexive way (mirror images of one another; 2HR),
and the most frequently used plane of symmetry is the midsaggital
(Mid) plane (2HRM). In figure 2.3 we see the cardinal directions for
2HRM signs.

We used only absolute directions in categorizing these signs
(**Away, Back, Contral, Down, Ipsil, Rear,** and **Up**). Given that
with 1H signs there was a single most common endpoint (**Ts**) and
given that with 2HIB signs there was a single most common endpoint (**Tb**), one might expect a single most common direction here,
too, and, in particular, one might expect it to be toward the Mid

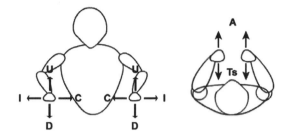

Figure 2.3. 2HRM Cardinal Directions
(U = **Up**; I = **Ipsil**; C = **Contral**; D = **Down**; A = **Away**;
Ts = Toward signer)

plane—which with 2HRM signs would be **Contral** (since, as we said, we categorized based on what the right hand does). This is not the most common direction, as our diagrams below will show. However, upon adding together the **Contral** and **Ipsil** signs, and then throwing in the **Contral-Ipsil** swing signs, it is easy to see that the most frequent direction of movement for these signs is, indeed, toward or away from the Mid plane. The same holds for signs with reflexive symmetry across other planes. In sum, in all three types of signs, across all five sign languages in the first part of this study, direction of movement is most strongly weighted by an obvious anchor or goal: for 1H signs, the signer; for 2HIB signs, the immobile base; for 2HR signs, the plane of symmetry.

Cataloging Curve Paths

We cataloged curve paths according to which plane the curve was defined in (that is, visible in) and whether the movement was CW or CCW. The three relevant planes were the Mid plane, the horizontal (HZ) plane (parallel to the ground), and the vertical wall (VW) plane (in front of the speaker, parallel to the signer's plane). We determined CW versus CCW on the Mid plane by looking at the hands from the right side of the signer; we made that determination on the HZ plane by looking down at the hands from above (even if the sign was made above the signer's eye level); we made that determination on the VW plane by looking at the hands from the signer's point of view.

Caveats on Cataloging

We have general caveats about our categorizations, which we will simply list.

1. If a sign holds a position at some point on the head or chest or other body location, including an immobile nondominant articulator, without a secondary movement in that position, we analyzed the movement that brought the dominant hand to that location as the primary movement. However, if a sign holds a position and does secondary movement or a handshape change in that position, and this secondary movement or hand-shape change did not also take place before or during the movement that brought the hand to that location, we analyzed the sign as having no primary movement (Perlmutter 1992). So a 1H sign that has finger wiggle that taps the chin, for example, has only secondary movement (as in the ASL sign COLOR); there is no path for this. But a 1H sign that holds an A-handshape at the forehead (as in the ASL sign STUPID/DUMB) has a path direction of **Ts**. Finally, if a sign consists of a handshape held in neutral space with no handshape change and no secondary movement, we analyzed it as having no movement whatsoever (these were rare: at most a couple per language, apart from numbers and manual alphabet letters). So a sign consisting of a 5-handshape held in neutral space, for example, has no movement. We give the number of such signs for each language in appendix A.

    If, instead, we had analyzed all signs as involving primary movement, the set of signs we labeled as having no primary movement in appendix A needs to be mined. Although some are made in neutral space, almost all of these 1H signs go into the **Ts** group (and we note that signs made on the head form the majority here). Almost all of these signs in the 2HIB category go into the **Tb** group. The rest of the signs, however, scatter by direction of path movement, and how they scatter depends on whether one analyzes signs close to the body as involving **Back**, signs held higher than midtorso as involving **Up**, and so on. We simply did not see any interesting results coming from such analyses. However, it is possible that defining particular points in space as target endpoints and classifying these signs according to at which target endpoint they perform their secondary movement or handshape change could yield interesting comparative information on the languages.

2. Often there is a question about whether a movement is secondary or primary. For example, in the LIS sign CURIOSO 'curious', the wrist nod makes the handshape go over the nose ridge from one side to the other, so that the elbow must lift a little, just because of physiology. Also, many speakers reduce primary movements to secondary movements quite liberally, at least in ASL. For example, in ASL the sign DESCRIBE/EXPLAIN is done with primary movement by some signers but secondary movement (wrist flexion) by others. In the hopes of making our study replicable, we adhered to our dictionaries, even if the version of the sign we are familiar with differs. However, on occasion it was difficult to distinguish what the dictionary was indicating, although the photographs were often accompanied by verbal descriptions of the movement. To make it more confusing, the BSL dictionary, which uses Stokoe notation in the caption of each photograph, sometimes has verbal descriptions inconsistent with the notation with regard to this particular issue. In such cases we consulted with informed people if possible (some signs were not known to the people we asked), or we tried to figure out which was the most physiologically natural or comfortable and then made a subjective decision.

3. Within 2HIB signs, distinguishing among **Tb, OnB**, and **PastB** is not always easy. If the dominant hand moves a significant

distance before making contact with the base, the contact is brief, and the hand continues to move a significant distance after that contact, it is clearly a **PastB** sign. But sometimes the movement path before or after contact may be minimal. And sometimes the contact may be extended, going across the palm and down the fingers, for example. None of our findings depends crucially on neat distinctions between **Tb, OnB**, and **PastB**, however. We include these distinctions in case future work should uncover their relevance.

4. In some photographs with 2HRM signs, it looks like the plane of symmetry has rotated 45° to the right or the left. We stayed true to the dictionary in most such cases. However, if we found that most such signs were photographs of a single signer (where the dictionary had photos of multiple signers), we checked against online sources. If we found that this was a peculiarity of the particular signer on those signs we were able to check, we assumed no plane rotation for any signs by that signer.

5. In the BSL dictionary we found one signer who consistently made 2HR signs off to one side or the other (not rotated—simply moved off to one side of her torso). After checking online when possible, we analyzed these as symmetrical across the Mid plane.

6. In Auslan we found some signs in which the left hand was dominant. All such photographs were of a single signer. We checked several signs against an online dictionary and found the right hand dominant. So we assumed this signer was left-handed and analyzed the signs accordingly.

7. In LSF we found signs in which the left hand was dominant. These were drawings rather than photographs, so we could not identify a particular signer. We checked whatever signs we could with an online source and with signers and determined that this must have simply been the dictionary's way of indicating that lefties use left as their dominant hand in signing, but not that some signs specifically called for left-hand dominance.

8. Sometimes the plane a curve was defined in seemed to be tilted, and there was no mention of the tilt in the dictionary. If we thought the tilt was due to physiological factors (that is, it was somewhat uncomfortable to make the specific movement entirely parallel to one of the three given planes), we discounted it (as with the sign LONG-AGO in BSL, #1480 in the dictionary). But if the tilt seemed physiologically arbitrary, then we kept note of it (as with the sign CIRCO / TEATRO 'circus / theater' in LIS).

9. The determination of whether a sign involves a curve is not always a simple matter. For example, if an A-hand moves downward in a straight path, that is easy to see. And if an A-hand moves in a large arc from point 1 to point 2, that is easy to see. But if an A-hand makes a wrist rotation as it moves downward in the shortest path from point 1 to point 2, the path will have a slight natural curve to it. Regarding curves due simply to secondary rotation, we classified the movement path as straight rather than curved. Likewise, we analyzed paths that involved one or several bounces from initial point to final point as not involving curves, since the slight arc of the path was a necessity of the hopping.

10. Sometimes a secondary movement (such as a wrist nod) or a change of handshape (such as from S-handshape to 1-handshape) will give the impression of a change of height. We disregard such complications. Only if there is a change in the height of the wrist do we indicate **Down** or **Up** (or in the height of the elbow, as in the sign SCOZIA 'Scotland' in LIS). The same is true for **Contral** or **Ipsil** movement. Likewise, if a hand moves from one point on the head to another point, and the shape of the path is necessarily affected by the shape of the head (as in the ASL sign DEAF), we disregard such complications. So, for example, the movement from temple to chin would be **Down** only, not **ContralDown**.

11. In our LSF dictionary, sometimes a repeat arrow was shorter than the arrow for the first movement. When we checked with

online sources, it did not seem to us that repeated movements in LSF were different from the other languages in this particular way. So we chose not to make a separate set for these.

Excluded Data

We excluded from our study signs in which we feared morphological effects might have undue prominence on the data, including the following: letters of the manual alphabet; ordinal numerals; signs with numeral incorporation; and compounds for which the component parts were phonetically identical to each independent word, their semantics were compositional, and we had already recorded the component parts. For the first two of these groups, this typically affected only the number of signs listed in the no-primary-movement group in appendix A.

We also excluded cardinal numbers. This was particularly important for LIS, since cardinal numbers have characteristics not found in other types of signs that could have thrown off our findings significantly. And, of course, since the cardinal numbers are unlimited, including them might have led to absurd results depending on how many the dictionary listed.

Regarding the exclusion of the above types of signs, we feel completely justified in our conclusion that including them would have led to no additional results of interest and might have kept us from seeing important phonetic generalizations.

However, in very few cases, we also excluded signs with aberrant movement characteristics in which these characteristics seemed pantomimic or otherwise patently nonarbitrary. This is a regrettably tricky area, because judging whether factors are pantomimic or nonarbitrary is a can of worms; depending on one's resourcefulness and imagination, the phonetic form of many signs might seem highly or, alternatively, barely motivated by semantics or pragmatics. So we did this only with very particular types of signs and very few signs, and we note below what effects this exclusion has on our data.

One type was signs with classifier incorporation, such as BOOK-SHELF in BSL (and many languages) and CASIER-À-BOUTEILLES 'rack for cylinders/bottles' in LSF, that is, signs that can include two or more independent movements, where one or both hands have the shape of a classifier and one or both hands either outline or locate an object with their movement. Likewise, we excluded a few signs with repeated movements (typically downward) that draw some action related to the referent, typically going from one side to the other (**Contral** or **Ipsil**), such as ENDUIRE 'smear' in LSF and BREAD (indicating the slices) in ASL. These signs, as well, could be analyzed as having incorporated a classifier predicate. There were fewer than ten of these in any given language (in fact, except for BSL and Auslan, there were fewer than five). Were we to include these, the small number of signs that we list in appendix A as possibly being polysyllabic would have doubled at most (depending on the language).

Another type was signs in which the movement draws the perimeter or outlines of the referent of the sign (which, arguably, are really examples of perimeter classifiers), such as HOUSE in many languages (with a slant down and away from the Mid plane and then a straight down movement), and signs that draw complete or partial boxes in the air typically with the 1-handshape, such as FRAME in many languages, or indicate the sides of cubes using a variety of handshapes such as BOX and ROOM in many languages. Were we to include these, the number of two-handed signs in which the hands move with reflexive symmetry across the Mid plane and signs that have what we call a "Z path shape" (that is, an angle—where ZZ indicates multiple angles, such as in a zigzag path) going in the direction of **DownIpsil** would have increased many times. Plus signs of the type that ROOM in ASL (and other languages) is typical of would have meant adding in a new glitch to our paths, since the hands either start glided (that is, with one hand ahead of the other along the plane of symmetry, rather than in an exact reflexive symmetry) and end up unglided, or start unglided and end up glided. Additionally, some of these signs (the very few that draw more than one corner with each hand) would have appeared in our list of possible polysyllabic signs in appendix A.

We also excluded signs that use aberrant movements while drawing a picture in the air of (some salient part of) the referent of the sign, such as mathematical symbols in many languages, punctuation signs in many languages, and signs such as TRAFFIC-LIGHT and ZEBRA-CROSSING in BSL, both of which include three very short separate movements. Were these signs included, new path shapes would have been added, particularly to 1H signs, and a few signs would have been added to our list of possible polysyllabic signs in appendix A, particularly for BSL and Auslan.

Finally, we excluded predicates that mimic the action in a phonetically complex way, where this mimicking is the same across the languages, such as SE-BOUTONNER 'button oneself up' in LSF. In fact, we think such signs belong more to the productive lexicon than to the fixed lexicon, since one could very well change the movement parameter if the buttons were arranged differently (in pairs, for example) or were of a remarkable size (very large or very tiny) or shape, and so on. In any case, the uniformity of such signs across the languages guarantees that their exclusion made no difference to the comparative statements we offer in this work.

We doubt that interesting comparative results would emerge from including any of the above types of signs for each language. Further, we note that the dictionaries were not all equally inclusive here: our BSL and LSF dictionaries, in particular, listed as single lexical items some signs that to us seemed to be descriptive phrases (see Johnston and Schembri 1999 for a discussion of this and other problems in signed language lexicography). To be fair, however, we note that the LSF dictionary was as much a grammar book as a dictionary. Further, different languages package information in different ways, and a single language can package the same information in multiple ways (compare 'fortnight' and 'two weeks' in English to the corresponding *quindicina* and *due settimane* in Italian). Given the complexity of the judgment of what a single lexical item is and what a phrase is and given that our dictionaries seem to have been using different standards for making this judgment, including these signs would have made these two languages appear to have more types of movement paths than the other three languages—a result that might have been misleading. Still, we note that the inclusion of these data would have significantly (in terms of numbers) affected only the group of signs we mention in appendix A as perhaps being polysyllabic. In light of this, we must stress that the study we offer here is of monosyllabic signs only.

This restriction raises the question of whether differences in frequency of monosyllabic versus polysyllabic signs in these five languages may have confounding effects in our study. In particular, it is generally agreed that ASL has mostly monosyllabic signs (Brentari 1998 and earlier studies cited therein), although we do not know of such claims about the other languages in this study. However, it has been argued that all sign languages make use of the syllable (Sandler and Lillo-Martin 2006) and, further, that the monosyllabic unit is the optimal form of the prosodic word in sign languages (Sandler 1999). Given that, we are hopeful that the proportion of monosyllables to polysyllables is relatively stable among noncompound signs across languages. Further, we note that the group of signs in appendix A is very small indeed, so the inclusion of these signs would not have made statistically significant differences in our findings.

Signs That Do Not Fit into Our Analyses

We also found certain types of signs that we could not insightfully include in our Venn diagrams and charts in the following chapters. Each type contained few signs, making comparative remarks difficult. They include the following:

1. Elbow signs. All the languages in our study have what we call "elbow signs." In these signs the nondominant hand makes continuous contact with the dominant elbow (on the elbow

crease, on the contralateral side, or on the bottom) while the dominant hand moves. In our corpora, ASL has thirteen elbow signs (two of these do not have primary movement); BSL, seven (six without primary movement); LIS, eleven; LSF, nine (six without primary movement); Auslan, eleven (six without primary movement); and ISN, three.

2. Fixed location/referent signs. These are signs in which the nondominant hand stays fixed in a certain position while the dominant hand moves independently of the nondominant. So, for example, the dominant hand might move **Up** but not up from the nondominant base, instead simply upward in neutral space. Generally these are mimetic signs (like shooting a gun or playing the guitar). In our corpora, ASL has one (and it is without primary movement); BSL, twelve (three without primary movement); LIS, five (one without primary movement); LSF, nine (three without primary movement); Auslan, nine (four without primary movement); and ISN, nine (two polysyllabic: PIRATA 'pirate' and FLECHA 'arrow'; two in which the nondominant hand makes a primary movement while the dominant hand stays still or only does secondary movement: MINA 'mine', FOCO 'spotlight'; and one that shows reflexivity over time). We suspect the rarity of these signs in our ASL data set is a random fault of our database.

3. Giant-Hand signs. There are some two-handed signs in which the hands have different handshapes and both move, but the hands are connected, so they move like one giant handshape (as in HELP or SHOW in ASL). For ASL we found twenty-one (two without primary movement) in our corpora; BSL, seventeen; LIS, five; LSF, seven; Auslan, thirteen (one without primary movement); and ISN, five. The large number in ASL relative to the size of the database is notable. (And recall that manual letters were excluded from our database—so BSL and Auslan two-handed manual alphabet letters are not included here.)

GATHERING THE DATA

4. Mismatched signs. Rare signs have two separate active hands
    that are mismatched. Either the hands have different shapes
    (as in TOTAL-COMMUNICATION in ASL) or the movements differ
    in path shape, length, direction, whether there is a secondary
    movement as well (as in OVERTAKE in BSL and SCULPTER
    'sculpt' in LSF), or whether both handshape and movement
    paths differ (as in TOAST in ASL and Auslan). Typically these
    signs mimic an action associated with their meaning (as in
    KARATE in various languages) or draw an outline in the air (like
    MONTAÑA 'mountain' in ISN). For ASL we found five in our
    corpora; BSL, zero (but there were some among the signs we
    excluded because they incorporated classifiers, such as OVER-
    TAKE); LSF, six; Auslan, four; and ISN, six. We suspect the
    absence of such signs in LIS is a random fault of our database.

5. Candidates for polysyllabic signs. Sometimes movement changes
    drastically within a sign, so that we may be dealing with two or
    more primary movements and, hence, two or more syllables.
    Most often these are instances of compounds (and we do not
    include compounds in our study as long as each of the compo-
    nent elements is already in the study). However, sometimes the
    phonological forms of the component elements of a compound
    differ enough from their phonological forms when they stand
    as separate lexical items that signers may not even be aware of
    their compound status; that is, they have been fully lexicalized.
    Others of these are mimetic signs. But, again, the transparency
    of a mimic depends largely not just on the experience of the
    particular signer but also on that person's imaginativeness. So
    we chose to be inclusive rather than exclusive with respect to
    assigning signs to this group. Still, we used only primary move-
    ment as our guide here.

    Had we considered secondary movement as well, the group
    would have been larger. For example, the sign DICE in Auslan
    has a secondary movement of shaking the dominant hand, then
    a primary movement **Contral** with a handshape change. The

sign mimics shaking and throwing dice. Another example from LSF is DIGESTIF 'after dinner liqueur', where a wrist rotation is followed by a primary movement **Down** and a handshape change, mimicking drinking followed by the liquid going down the esophagus. Signs like these could well be polysyllabic, but since only one primary movement is involved, we chose to include such signs in our tables of regular monosyllabic signs in appendices B and C. We note that several of these signs would have been analyzable as signs with a primary movement angle path or as swing signs but for the fact that they do something on one or both sides of the angle or during the different phases of the swing that makes the sides or phases unequal. Lists of candidates for polysyllabic signs in our corpora are given in appendix A.

6. Pseudo-Reflexive signs. Among the candidates for polysyllabic signs, we found a subset that we extracted and list here because of their special phonetic shape (which is semantically motivated). A few 1H signs are remarkable in that they do a certain action with the dominant hand moving **Ipsil** (or some combination that involves **Ipsil**) and then repeat that action with the dominant hand moving **Contral** (or some combination that involves **Contral**). It is as though they are trying to be signs that are reflexive across the Mid plane, just with a single hand rather than two. In LIS we found QUALCHE-VOLTA 'sometimes', and in LSF we found VOYAGER 'travel' and ROUGE-À-LÈVRES 'lipstick'. Some 2HIB signs are similar, moving the dominant hand **Ipsil** (or some combination of **Ipsil**) then **Contral** (or some combination of **Contral**). In ASL we found CANCEL; in LIS, ANNULARE 'cancel'; and in Auslan, AXE, DISCRIMINATION, and DISQUALIFIED.

3

Analysis of Signs with Noncurve Paths in ASL, BSL, LIS, LSF, and Auslan

The raw data that form the basis for the Venn diagrams, charts, and statistics in this chapter are presented in the tables in appendix B.

General Remarks on Analysis

Here and in all the analyses in later chapters, we give numbers and percentages, organized into charts, tables, and diagrams. We also give statistics. Originally, we had not intended to offer statistical evidence, for the very reason that we did not consider it necessary. Since we used entire dictionaries, there is a sense (the dictionary sense) in which our corpora are complete, our sampling being of the entire population. As opposed to random sampling, the use of entire dictionaries can be likened to interpreting data from a census—for all intents and purposes, the sample size is nearly all encompassing and, as such, should be representative of any relationships that are drawn from the data. That is, our data, like a census, are the best available attempts at cataloging every sign.

In fact, of course, no dictionary is ever complete. And some of our dictionaries had different goals from others. For example, our LSF dictionary was intended to teach the reader to sign, thus some of the signs involved matters of agreement and others involved productive (as opposed to frozen) signs (and therefore fell into our excluded data). For this reason, we did, in the end, run statistical analyses. The very size of our corpora, huge in comparison with most phonetic studies, makes a statistical approach not only possible but also more likely to ensure the integrity of our conclusions.

We operate under the assumption that the dictionaries we used present randomly selected corpora. Hopefully, all dictionaries are random. Further, none of the dictionaries gave any statement on the selection of the lexical items included, so the default situation behind such a lack of statement should be that these large data sets were randomly composed. Importantly, this assumption is the only one that allows us to proceed with a statistical analysis, since only under this assumption can the data set be taken to be representative of the languages.

We performed chi-square statistical analysis on much of the data. Sometimes the differences in a data set just barely make the cutoff for being statistically significant (that is, the p-value is just barely less than .05). We are hesitant to draw conclusions from such statistics. Yet we realize that others may recognize important trends that would have otherwise been missed if we had not included the statistics. In the interest of our work being as complete and useful as possible, we present all statistics we think might have a chance of being linguistically relevant. The p-values we give throughout the book indicate the strength of the evidence we have against the null hypothesis: that the observed data are different from the expected data. As shorthand for this, when we give p-values, we talk about the percentage chance of the data being drawn from an identical corpus.

Additionally, our data from multiple languages sometimes show very little variation and, accordingly, a great chance of being drawn from a single language (maybe in the ninetieth percentile or higher), while at other times they show considerable, although not statistically relevant, variation, exhibiting a relatively low chance of being drawn from a single language (maybe in the tenth percentile or lower—whereas only less than 5% is statistically significant). Nevertheless, if the differences are not statistically significant, we do not draw on them in chapter 6, where we form our conclusions and make hypotheses. Still, we set all the data before our readers in the interim chapters, in case they should see relevant generalizations that our statistically based approach misses.

We organized the signs with paths other than curves according to the direction of the movement path. By plotting the distributions on Venn diagrams, we were able to establish general distribution patterns of movement while making the data visually accessible. Using VennMaster (Kestler et al. 2008), a tool used to establish analogous relationships in gene regulation, we created area-proportional diagrams in which the size of each circle in relationship to other circles in that set indicates the number of signs that belong to a specific category. That is, the diagram is scaled accurately to reflect the relative occurrence of signs within a particular movement category. The intersections of the diagrams show where movement directions can be combined in the movement path.

For ease of expostulation, we call the degree of overlapping particular to a movement direction its "adaptive modularity." A movement direction that combines with several other directions, such as **Away** (as we will see below), is said to have high adaptive modularity. On the Venn diagrams, this is depicted by the amount and size of overlappings between various circles.

We discuss one-handed noncurve signs, then two-handed non-curve signs with an immobile base, then two-handed noncurve signs exhibiting reflexive symmetry across the Mid plane, omitting entirely any consideration of swing signs. Rather, we postpone the discussion of swing signs until after the discussion of all three types, so that we can point out generalizations about swing signs that cut across the types of signs.

One-Handed Signs (1H)

Figures 3.1 through 3.5 give the Venn diagrams for 1H signs with noncurve movement paths, and illustration 3.1 gives a sample sign. We lump all such signs into one group, thus diverging from

ANALYSIS OF SIGNS WITH NONCURVE PATHS

Battison's (1978) typology of signs. Battison separates 1H signs into two groups: those articulated in free space without contact with a body part (what he calls "Type 0 signs") and those in which the hand makes contact with some portion of the body (other than the opposite hand; what he calls "Type X signs"). Battison's Type X signs are subsumed under our 1H signs with the direction **Ts**.

Illustration 3.1. DRINK in ASL, Example of 1H Noncurve Sign

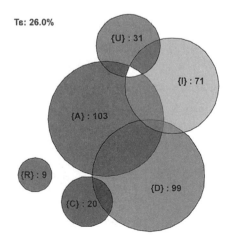

Figure 3.1. ASL 1H Noncurve Signs
(A = **Away**; U = **Up**; I = **Ipsil**; D = **Down**; C = **Contral**; R = **Rear**)

ANALYSIS OF SIGNS WITH NONCURVE PATHS

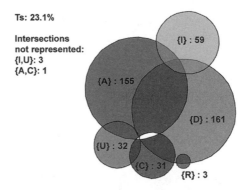

Ts: 23.1%

Intersections
not represented:
{I,U}: 3
{A,C}: 1

Figure 3.2. BSL 1H Noncurve Signs

(A = **Away**; U = **Up**; I = **Ipsil**; D = **Down**; C = **Contral**; R = **Rear**)

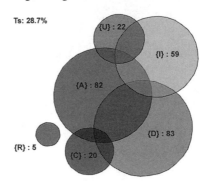

Ts: 28.7%

Figure 3.3. LIS 1H Noncurve Signs

(A = **Away**; U = **Up**; I = **Ipsil**; D = **Down**; C = **Contral**; R = **Rear**)

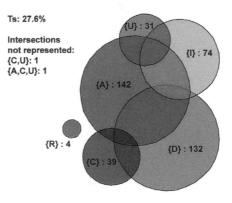

Ts: 27.6%

Intersections
not represented:
{C,U}: 1
{A,C,U}: 1

Figure 3.4. LSF 1H Noncurve Signs

(A = **Away**; U = **Up**; I = **Ipsil**; D = **Down**; C = **Contral**; R = **Rear**)

ANALYSIS OF SIGNS WITH NONCURVE PATHS

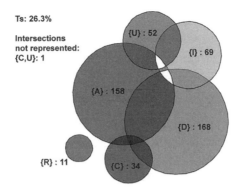

Ts: 26.3%

Intersections
not represented:
{C,U}: 1

{U} : 52

{I} : 69

{A} : 158

{D} : 168

{R} : 11

{C} : 34

Figure 3.5. Auslan 1H Noncurve Signs

(A = **Away**; U = **Up**; I = **Ipsil**; D = **Down**; C = **Contral**; R = **Rear**)

The uniformity of adaptive modularity of path directions across the languages is striking. The relative relationships of the **Away, Down, Ipsil,** and **Up** "core" remain more or less fixed. **Away** has the greatest adaptive modularity, combining in our corpora with **Down, Ipsil, Up**, and **Contral** in all the languages except ASL, where **Contral** is an exception. In fact, in our corpora in ASL **Contral** is aberrant, in combining only with one other direction (**Down**); in LIS it combines with two directions (**Away** and **Down**); and in BSL, LSF, and Auslan it combines with three directions (**Away, Down,** and **Up**).

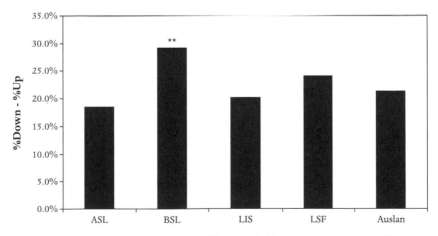

Figure 3.6. 1H Noncurve Signs: Difference in Percentage between **Down** and **Up** Signs ($\chi^2 = 15.8$; **$p < .005$)

ANALYSIS OF SIGNS WITH NONCURVE PATHS

A different analytical approach to the same database, however, reveals interesting trends. First, across four of the languages, the difference in the percentage of signs that are **Down** and those that are **Up** is constant, between 19% and 24% (with **Down** being more prevalent; figure 3.6). BSL statistically differs with high significance (indicated by the double asterisk before the p) from the other four languages, with the gap between **Down** and **Up** reaching 29.2% ($\chi^2 = 15.8$; $^{\star\star}p < .005$).

Second, the difference in the percentage of signs that are **Ipsil** and those that are **Contral** splits in an interesting way (figure 3.7): **Ipsil** is favored heavily over **Contral** (approximately 13%) in ASL and LIS, whereas it is only slightly favored (approximately 7%) in Auslan, BSL, and LSF. This split is clearly along neither genetic nor origin-bound/diaspora lines, since ASL and LIS fall together genetically, but LSF is left out, and ASL and LIS fall together as diaspora languages, but Auslan is left out.

Third, the difference in the percentage of signs that are **Away** and those that are **Ts** is remarkably greater in BSL and highly significantly greater in LSF than in the diaspora languages (figure 3.8).

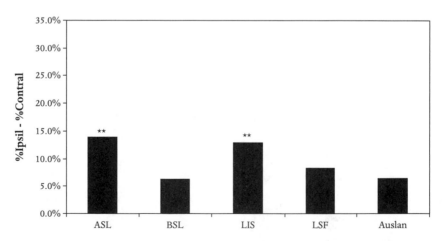

Figure 3.7. 1H Noncurve Signs: Difference in Percentage between **Ipsil** and **Contral** Signs ($\chi^2 = 24.6$; $^{\star\star}p < .001$ for ASL compared with others and for LIS compared with others)

ANALYSIS OF SIGNS WITH NONCURVE PATHS

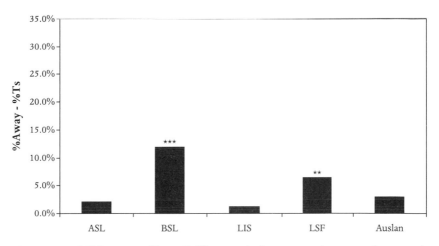

Figure 3.8. 1H Noncurve Signs: Difference in Percentage between **Away** and **Ts** Signs ($\chi^2 = 63.6$; **$p < .005$ for LSF compared with others; ***$p < .0001$ for BSL compared with others)

In terms of the overall geography of the intersections, BSL and LSF are the most similar to each other, the only difference being in the relative size of the various intersections. In both languages all physiologically easily combinable directions (for 1H these are **Away, Contral, Down, Ipsil,** and **Up**) do combine with at least three other directions, whereas **Away** combines with all four. The uncombinable directions are **Ts** (by definition) and **Rear** (by physiological ease), with the exception that in two BSL signs **Rear** combines with **Down**. So high activity in combining in 1H signs is a characteristic that sets BSL and LSF apart from the others. Here we see for the first time the clustering that made us adopt the terms "origin-bound" for BSL and LSF and "diaspora" for the other three languages, as discussed in chapter 1 in the section "Import of This Work."

ASL and LIS are likewise very similar to each other; the difference is that in LIS the combinations **AwayContralDown** and **AwayIpsilUp** are allowed, whereas they are not found in ASL in our corpora. The distributions of combinations in BSL and LSF are also very similar to each other; the difference is that in LSF **Contral** can combine with **Away-Down** and **Away-Up** and we also find

AwayIpsilUp. Auslan more closely resembles ASL and LIS with respect to combinability—although it lacks **AwayIpsilUp,** and the adaptive modularity of **Contral** is more like that of BSL—so, again, we find these three languages clustering together as a diaspora in contrast to the two origin-bound languages.

Statistical Significance

Chi-square statistical analysis on the entire data sets regarding 1H signs presented thus far in this chapter shows that with respect to several path directions, the differences between the languages are not significant. Thus, for **Ts** ($\chi^2 = 3.6$; $p = .46$), **Contral** ($\chi^2 = 5.3$; $p = .25$), **Up** ($\chi^2 = 2.7$; $p = .61$), and **Rear** ($\chi^2 = 6.0$; $p = .20$), we see no strong contrasts among the languages.

However, for **Away** the p-value is .0555 ($\chi^2 = 9.2$), which approaches statistical significance. So we did further tests. When comparing only ASL and BSL, we find a significant difference ($\chi^2 = 4.4$; $^*p < .05$). So the (quite casual) claim we observed at the international Deaf conference at Swarthmore College in March 2008 (the claim that started our whole study)—that BSL signs move away from the signer much more frequently than do ASL signs—turns out to be true for 1H signs.

We ran further statistics to see if with respect to **Away** the languages clustered around genetic lines. Because the differences in the LSF, LIS, and ASL family approached statistical significance ($\chi^2 = 4.8$; $p = .09$) and the differences in the BSL and Auslan family even more closely approached statistical significance ($\chi^2 = 3.7$; $p = .054$), we cannot conclude whether we have a genetic split with respect to **Away**, although the data are tending toward the conclusion that we do not.

At this point a note about statistics is in order. A p-value of less than .05 indicates significant difference (that is, there is less than a 5% chance that the data are all drawn from a common group—so, statistically speaking, the group is not coherent); a p-value of less than .005 indicates a highly significant difference (less than a half percent chance that the data are coherent); a p-value of less than .0005 indicates an extremely highly significant difference (less than a one twentieth percent chance that the data are coherent). Our data samples are extremely large, so there is every reason to rely on the statistical analyses we give of this corpus. So if the p-value is .06, we will not consider a group to be incoherent, even though it is very close to being so. This may feel strange to our readers—and for good reason. As we noted at the outset, our data sampling is not really random. Since we used entire dictionaries, our data sampling could (in some rarified world in which dictionaries were truly complete) be considered total, in which case a p-value of .06 indicates less coherence than a p-value of .16 and far less coherence than a p-value of .72, for example. So, although we will stick to the statistics (in the knowledge that dictionaries are never truly complete, and ours are no exception), we consistently point out the wide range of p-values and consider them when evaluating the conclusions the statistics lead us to.

Let us return now to our analyses. We also ran further statistics to see if perhaps with respect to **Away** the languages clustered around the origin-bound/diaspora split. In fact, a comparison of BSL and LSF with respect to **Away** shows a 75% certainty that the two languages are the same ($\chi^2 = 0.1$; $p = .75$), whereas a comparison of ASL, LSF, and LIS shows an 82% certainty that the three languages are the same ($\chi^2 = 0.4$; $p = .82$).

Turning to the use of the direction **Down**, we find that the languages certainly differ significantly ($\chi^2 = 10.8$; $^\star p < .05$). So we performed further tests, looking first to see if the languages clustered along genetic lines. In fact, ASL, LIS, and LSF appear to be similar ($\chi^2 = 2.4$; $p = .31$). And, interestingly (perhaps shockingly to some), Auslan and BSL differ significantly ($\chi^2 = 5.0$; $^\star p < .05$). As to the origin-bound versus diaspora split, we find evidence that ASL, Auslan, and LIS cluster together with regard to **Down** ($\chi^2 = 0.9$; $p = .64$). A comparison of BSL and LSF with respect to **Down** also shows a clustering ($\chi^2 = 2.2$; $p = .14$).

Finally, turning to the use of the direction **Ipsil**, the languages differ quite significantly (χ^2 = 13.4; $^\star p$ < .05). Additional testing revealed a strong genetic tendency: ASL, LIS, and LSF show a 77% chance that the languages are the same (χ^2 = 0.5; p = .77), whereas BSL and Auslan show an 80% chance of being the same (χ^2 = 0.1; p = .80).

Although our previous analyses on the origin-bound/diaspora split revealed patterns in the **Away** and **Down** directions, we find that the diaspora daughters, ASL, LIS, and Auslan, have very little similarity with each other with respect to **Ipsil** (χ^2 = 9.8; $^\star p$ < .05). The origin-bound daughters, BSL and LSF, approach statistical significance (χ^2 = 3.2; p = .08). Therefore, it appears that with respect to **Ipsil** these languages cluster on genetics more strongly than on the origin-bound/diaspora split.

The Goal and Its Motivation

The fact that 1H signs should have such a strong tendency to move in the direction **Ts** begs for an explanation. It looks like 1H signs favor a common anchor, if you will, for the goal of the movement. Is this a prosodic matter, where perhaps the anchor (the signer's body) allows a clear final hold (even if short)? Or is this perhaps physiological, where a goal with a tactile reality (the body) is somehow preferable to a goal without one (a point in space)?

In studies of deaf children's sign language acquisition, tactile information has been shown to aid language development (Boyes-Braem 1990). The hearing child acquiring spoken language has constant aural feedback on her language production. The deaf child acquiring sign language often makes signs outside the visual field of the signer (since the signer's eyes are not generally on her own articulators), thus she does not have constant visual feedback on her language production. Nevertheless, the signer does have feedback in the form of proprioception, that is, feedback from the internal state of the body. With our eyes closed, we can know what our hands are doing and where they are; we can coordinate our movements impressively. But it has been shown that if the production of a sign also gives the signer tactile feedback, this can lead to self-correction that results in earlier accurate production. Perhaps the tactile information at the end of most 1H **Ts** signs (since most are contact signs) is favored precisely because such signs are easier to acquire than signs that do not give tactile feedback.

That signs can favor or disfavor certain types of anchors has been argued elsewhere. Signs that are made from a single manual letter in BSL (such as MOTHER, which is a repetition of the letter M) strongly favor manual letters in which the nondominant hand has a large surface area, like M, N, H, F, and G, whereas letters where the surface area of the nondominant hand is small are disfavored, so you do not get many S, U, or P single manual letter signs (Sutton-Spence 1994). Likewise, in 2HIB signs in ASL the vastly favored handshape for the nondominant hand is B, accounting for almost 60% of such signs (Napoli and Wu 2003). Since a larger surface area allows more tactile feedback, perhaps these findings support our account of why **Ts** is the prevalent anchor for 1H signs.

Two-Handed Signs with One Hand Being an Immobile Base (2HIB)

Figures 3.9 through 3.13 give the Venn diagrams for two-handed signs with an immobile base and noncurve movement paths, and an example of such a sign is shown in illustration 3.2. Again, we lump all 2HIB signs into one group, thus diverging from Battison's (1978) typology. He separates 2HIB signs into two groups: those in which both hands are specified for the same handshape (which he calls "Type 2 signs") and those in which the hands have different handshapes (which he calls "Type 3 signs"). He notes that when the hands have different handshapes, there are restrictions on which handshapes are allowed (noted under his dominance condition). Since handshape is not a focus of our study, we have conflated the two types.

ANALYSIS OF SIGNS WITH NONCURVE PATHS

Illustration 3.2. KNOCK in ASL, Example of 2HIB Noncurve Sign

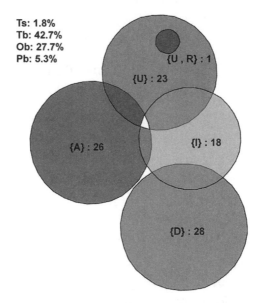

Figure 3.9. ASL 2HIB Noncurve Signs
(A = **Away**; U = **Up**; I = **Ipsil**; D = **Down**; R = **Rear**; **OnB** = On the base;
PastB = Past the base)

ANALYSIS OF SIGNS WITH NONCURVE PATHS

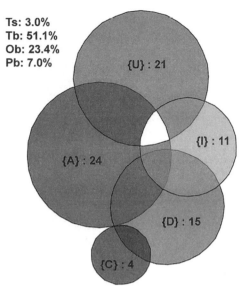

Ts: 3.0%
Tb: 51.1%
Ob: 23.4%
Pb: 7.0%

{U} : 21

{I} : 11

{A} : 24

{D} : 15

{C} : 4

Figure 3.10. BSL 2HIB Noncurve Signs
(A = **Away**; U = **Up**; I = **Ipsil**; D = **Down**; **OnB** = On the base;
PastB = Past the base)

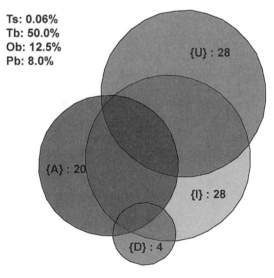

Ts: 0.06%
Tb: 50.0%
Ob: 12.5%
Pb: 8.0%

{U} : 28

{A} : 20

{I} : 28

{D} : 4

Figure 3.11. LIS 2HIB Noncurve Signs
(A = **Away**; U = **Up**; I = **Ipsil**; D = **Down**; **OnB** = On the base;
PastB = Past the base)

ANALYSIS OF SIGNS WITH NONCURVE PATHS

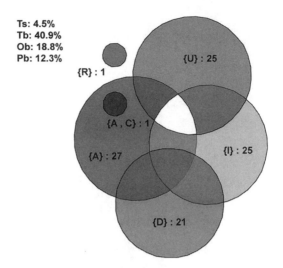

Ts: 4.5%
Tb: 40.9%
Ob: 18.8%
Pb: 12.3%

{R} : 1

{U} : 25

{A , C} : 1

{A} : 27

{I} : 25

{D} : 21

Figure 3.12. LSF 2HIB Noncurve Signs

(A = **Away**; U = **Up**; I = **Ipsil**; D = **Down**; R = **Rear**; **OnB** = On the base;

PastB = Past the base)

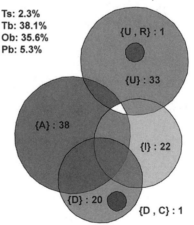

Ts: 2.3%
Tb: 38.1%
Ob: 35.6%
Pb: 5.3%

{U , R} : 1

{U} : 33

{A} : 38

{I} : 22

{D} : 20

{D , C} : 1

Figure 3.13. Auslan 2HIB Noncurve Signs

(A = **Away**; U = **Up**; I = **Ipsil**; D = **Down**; R = **Rear**; C = **Contral**;

OnB = On the base; **PastB** = Past the base)

Immediately one notes that in our corpora **Contral** does not even appear in ASL and LIS, whereas it appears on only one sign in LSF (in combination with **Away**) and in Auslan (in combination with **Down**). In BSL, however, it appears uncombined as well as

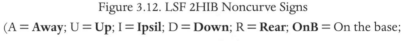

combined. Clearly this paucity is because **Tb** subsumes most **Contral** signs. Since the number of signs involved is so small, nothing statistical can be concluded—a fact we are grateful for, since we know of one such sign in ASL, which just happens to be missing from our corpora: GO-OFF-TOPIC.

We further note, without additional comment, that LIS has few **Down** signs compared with the other languages.

Another immediate difference that pops out is that overall adaptive modularity is lower for most directions than it is with 1H signs. In our corpora **Down** combines with only **Ipsil** in ASL and with only **Ipsil** and **Away** in the others, with the exception that in BSL and Auslan we find **Back** also combining with **Contral** in a single sign in each language. Likewise, **Up** combines with only two other directions (**Away** and **Ipsil**) in all languages, with the exception that in ASL and Auslan we find **Up** also combining with **Rear** in a single sign in each language. In all languages if three directions combine (which does not happen in ASL in our corpora, but does in the other four), **Away** must be involved; so we find **AwayDown-Ipsil** in four languages plus **AwayIpsil-Up** in LIS. Auslan allows the most combining of directions, and ASL allows the least.

In BSL and Auslan, **Away** has the highest adaptive modularity based on the percentage of signs it combines with (just as we found with 1H signs); however, in ASL, LIS, and LSF, **Ipsil** has the highest adaptive modularity (although for LSF this is only by a difference of one sign with respect to **Away**). So the split here is along genetic lines.

Let's now take an overview of the signs that are directed toward, on, or past the base where the relevant comparisons and percentages are given in table 3.1, and where those percentages are with respect to the total number of 2HIB signs. (To get the comparison of **Tb** cf. **OnB**, for example, divide the difference between the number of **Tb** and **OnB** signs by the number of **OnB** signs. Note that **Tb** is greater than **OnB** in the given proportion.) (Note that the

ANALYSIS OF SIGNS WITH NONCURVE PATHS

TABLE 3.1. 2HIB Noncurve Signs Excluding Swings

	Tb	OnB	PastB	Sum (Tb, OnB, PastB)	Tb cf. OnB	OnB cf. PastB
ASL	43%	28%	5%	76%	0.54	4.25
BSL	51%	23%	7%	81%	1.18	2.35
LIS	50%	13%	8%	70%	3.00	0.57
LSF	41%	19%	12%	72%	1.17	0.53
Auslan	39%	36%	5%	79%	0.06	5.73

discrepancy between the percentage in column 4 and the sums of the percentages in the first three columns for LIS and Auslan are a result of rounding to the nearest percentage in the first three columns.) The directions **Tb, OnB**, and **PastB** are, of course, unable to be combined by definition. Adding together the **Tb, OnB**, and **PastB** sets, we find that in all the languages at least 70% and as high as 81% of the 2HIB signs (with a noncurve path and excluding swing signs) are subsumed here. This should come as no surprise, since the nondominant articulator serves as a base for the dominant hand; it is the goal or anchor, just as the signer's body is the anchor for 1H signs.

In all the languages **Tb** is larger than **OnB**, although here we find huge differences. In Auslan it is only by 6%, whereas in LIS it is by 300%. Additionally, **OnB** is larger than **PastB** in all the languages, but again the ratios vary hugely. LIS and LSF are on the low side, and all the other languages are at a minimum four times greater, with Auslan being ten times greater. Since **Tb** signs almost all make contact with the base and **OnB** signs do all make contact, whereas only some **PastB** signs do, we conclude that, as with 1H signs, the tendency to have a physically concrete goal that gives tactile feedback is strong across the languages. Nevertheless, we note that in our corpora Auslan does stand out among these languages as the one that makes almost as great use of **OnB** as **Tb**, and LIS stands out (though not as boldly) as being the one with the strongest preference for **Tb** over **OnB**.

ANALYSIS OF SIGNS WITH NONCURVE PATHS

Statistical Significance

Chi-square statistical analysis on the entire data set regarding 2HIB signs presented thus far in this chapter shows that, with respect to a number of path directions, the differences between the languages are not great. So for **Away** ($\chi^2 = 4.9$; $p = .30$), **Contral** ($\chi^2 = 7.9$; $p = .10$), and **Rear** ($\chi^2 = 1.6$; $p = .82$), the languages do not show significant contrasts. Additionally, they do not show clusterings either.

However, for **Up** there is a highly significant difference ($\chi^2 = 22.2$; **$p < .005$). LIS shows a much stronger presence of **Up** than the other languages (15.9% vs. a range of 5.6% to 8.1%).

Likewise, for **Ipsil** there is an extremely highly significant difference among the languages ($\chi^2 = 41.8$; ***$p < .0001$). LIS and, to a lesser extent, LSF make strong use of **Ipsil** in contrast to the other three languages.

Additionally, for **Down** there is a significant difference among the languages ($\chi^2 = 10.7$; *$p < .05$). ASL is significantly different from all the other languages (compared with BSL, $\chi^2 = 3.9$; *$p < .05$; with Auslan, $\chi^2 = 4.4$; *$p < .05$; with LIS, $\chi^2 = 5.8$; *$p < .05$) except for LSF, with which it has a 77% chance of being the same ($\chi^2 = 0.1$). BSL and Auslan also pattern together, with a 95% chance of being the same (and no significant difference with LIS or LSF). The outlier here is LIS, which disfavors **Down** more strongly than any of the others. Unexpectedly, LIS significantly contrasts with ASL and with LSF (compared with LSF, $\chi^2 = 4.7$; *$p < .05$) but not with BSL ($\chi^2 = 1.1$; $p = .29$) or Auslan ($\chi^2 = 1.3$; $p = .26$).

Finally, we looked at the directions that went toward, on, or over the base hand. When we looked at the preference for **OnB** over **PastB,** we found an extremely highly significant difference among the languages ($\chi^2 = 101.0$; ***$p < .0001$). LIS and LSF cluster here ($\chi^2 = 0.8$; $p = .38$), but the other three languages do not ($\chi^2 = 22.8$; ***$p < .0001$). On the other hand, we found highly significant differences across the languages when we split these signs up into the three groups of **Tb** ($\chi^2 = 18.5$; **$p < .005$), **OnB** ($\chi^2 = 50.2$; **$p < .005$), and **PastB** ($\chi^2 = 16.9$; **$p < .005$). No patterns emerged, however; it simply looked as if each language did its own thing. We then combined all three groups into one big group of signs anchored on the base hand. Again, there were significant differences ($\chi^2 = 13.9$; $^\star p < .05$), and the languages clustered along genetic lines. The BSL and Auslan data have a 38% chance of being identical ($\chi^2 = 0.8$).

The Goal

The grouping together of **Tb, OnB,** and **PastB** signs allows us to see the strong propensity of 2HIB signs toward a specific goal: the base hand. That base hand acts as the anchor again. Since contact is typical in these signs, the anchor provides tactile feedback for the signer. Thus the motivation for this goal is open to the same account we suggested for the goal of 1H signs.

Two-Handed Signs with Reflexive Symmetry across the Midsaggital Plane (2HRM)

Two-handed signs in which both hands move strongly favor reflexive symmetry across the Mid plane, a well-known fact (Napoli and Wu 2003, building on Battison 1974, 1978 and Liddell and Johnson 1989). Figures 3.14 through 3.18 give the Venn diagrams for such signs, and an example is seen in illustration 3.3. The distribution of overlapping

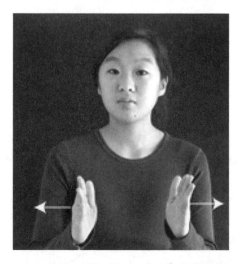

Illustration 3.3. WIDE in ASL, Example of 2HRM Noncurve Sign

ANALYSIS OF SIGNS WITH NONCURVE PATHS

Intersections not represented:

{B,D}: 2
{C,U}: 2

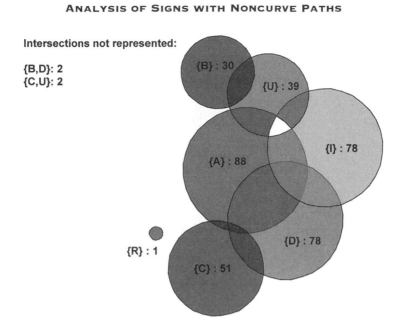

Figure 3.14. ASL 2HRM Noncurve Signs

(A = **Away**; U = **Up**; I = **Ipsil**; D = **Down**; C = **Contral**; R = **Rear**; B = **Back**)

Intersections not represented:

{A,C}: 4
{A,I}: 8
{A,U}: 4
{C,U}: 4
{B,C,U}: 1

*N.B. The {A,D} intersection is overrepresented in order to limit the number of intersections unrepresented.

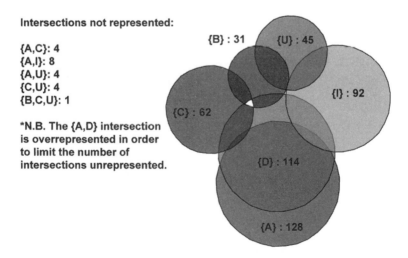

Figure 3.15. BSL 2HRM Noncurve Signs

(A = **Away**; U = **Up**; I = **Ipsil**; D = **Down**; C = **Contral**; B = **Back**)

ANALYSIS OF SIGNS WITH NONCURVE PATHS

Intersections not represented:

{D,I}: 5
{I,U}: 13

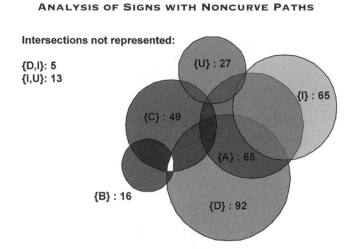

Figure 3.16. LIS 2HRM Noncurve Signs

(A = **Away**; U = **Up**; I = **Ipsil**; D = **Down**; C = **Contral**; B = **Back**)

Intersections not represented:

{B,C}: 1
{B,D}: 2
{C,U}: 3

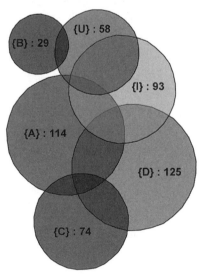

Figure 3.17. LSF 2HRM Noncurve Signs

(A = **Away**; U = **Up**; I = **Ipsil**; D = **Down**; C = **Contral**; B = **Back**)

ANALYSIS OF SIGNS WITH NONCURVE PATHS

Intersections not represented:

{C,U}: 5
{B,C,D}: 1

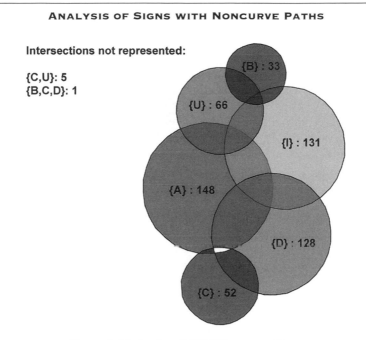

Figure 3.18. Auslan 2HRM Noncurve Signs

(A = **Away**; U = **Up**; I = **Ipsil**; D = **Down**; C = **Contral**; B = **Back**)

sections is very similar across the languages. **Away** has the greatest adaptive modularity, combining with every direction possible; only the physically impossible combinations of **Back** and **Rear** are excluded.

Contral, Down, Ipsil, and **Up** interact in predictable ways: **Up** overlaps with **Ipsil,** which overlaps with **Down,** which overlaps with **Contral,** which overlaps with **Up,** and all overlap with **Away.**

The biggest differences in the languages are in the combinability of **Back. Back** combines with **Contral, Down, Ipsil,** and **Up** in Auslan, with **Contral, Down,** and **Up** in BSL and LSF, but in LIS it combines only with **Contral** and **Down,** and in ASL it combines only with **Down** and **Up.**

Thus the Venn diagrams do not help us notice major differences. However, using the same approach of percentage differences that we used on 1H signs, we find that LIS favors **Down** over **Up** more heavily than do the other languages (figure 3.19) and that Auslan favors **Ipsil** over **Contral** more heavily than do the other languages (figure 3.20).

ANALYSIS OF SIGNS WITH NONCURVE PATHS

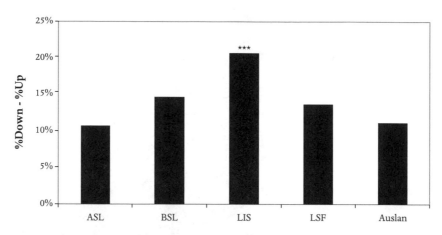

Figure 3.19. 2HRM Noncurve Signs: Difference in Percentage between **Down** and **Up** Signs ($\chi^2 = 24.4$; ***$p < .0001$ for LIS compared with others)

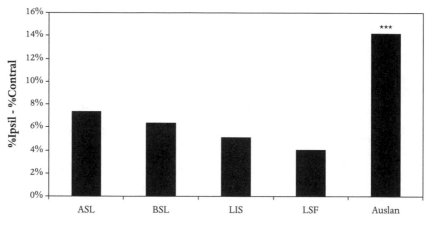

Figure 3.20. 2HRM Noncurve Signs: Difference in Percentage between **Ipsil** and **Contral** Signs ($\chi^2 = 50.6$; ***$p < .0001$)

Statistical Significance

Chi-square statistical analysis on the entire data set for 2HRM noncurve signs presented thus far in this chapter shows once more that with respect to a number of path directions, the differences between the languages are not great. So for **Away** ($\chi^2 = 3.6$; $p = .46$), **Back** ($\chi^2 = 2.8$; $p = .59$), **Up** ($\chi^2 = 3.1$; $p = .54$), and **Ipsil** ($\chi^2 = 3.7$; $p = .44$), the languages do not show significant contrasts, nor do they show clusterings along genetic or diaspora lines.

However, for **Contral** there is a significant contrast ($\chi^2 = 13.4$; $*p < .05$). The languages turn out to cluster along genetic lines here, with the LSF, LIS, and ASL family exhibiting a 59% chance of being the same ($\chi^2 = 1.1$; $p = .59$), and the BSL and Auslan family exhibiting a 46% chance of being the same ($\chi^2 = 4.0$; $p = .46$).

We also find a significant difference for **Down** ($\chi^2 = 12.4$; $*p < .05$). Here the languages do not cluster. Instead, LIS stands out as having a strong preference for **Down.**

And, finally, chi-square statistical analysis on the data in figure 3.20 shows us an extremely highly statistically significant difference ($\chi^2 = 50.6$; $***p < .0001$). Auslan looks like the disruptive figure here. Upon removing Auslan from the data set, we find that the other four languages are similar, although not very; the differences approach statistical significance ($\chi^2 = 7.1$; $p = .07$). Notice that the p-value has changed by more than a power of 2. So Auslan's favoring of **Ipsil** over **Contral** is statistically significant.

A note on statistics is pertinent at this point. In classical statistics the removal of outliers after doing an analysis is taboo. Traditionally statisticians would screen the data beforehand, remove any obvious outliers (and, of course, check the source of the data to see whether these obvious outliers were improperly recorded), and then proceed with analysis. With huge sample sizes, however, that type of screening is impractical. So a different approach to statistics, "robust statistics," came up with a way of identifying outliers after analysis and then removing them from the database, allowing a second analysis without them (Rousseeuw and Leroy 2003; Huber 2004). It is important to follow the prescribed methods of robust analysis to avoid common pitfalls, such as multiple outliers interacting and masking each other, or removing a large outlier with the result that another outlier (that should also be removed) now looks relatively normal and so is left in the data pool. These problems are more severe the larger and more complex the database.

The database on favoring **Ipsil** over **Contral** is relatively small, however—small enough that manual (or visual) detection of Auslan as the outlier is possible and reliable. We could have pointed out this outlier initially and removed it from the database (more in line with classical approaches), but we instead chose to present the statistics on the whole group first and then on the group minus the outlier for the sake of clarity in exposition.

We will continue to identify and handle outliers this way in the rest of the book, particularly in chapter 4, in which the data for curves is so small that visual detection of outliers is quite simple.

The Goal

We postpone a discussion of the goal in 2HRM noncurve signs until after our discussion of swing signs.

Swing Signs

The raw data on swing signs are found in appendix B. Relative percentages are given in table 3.2 (where we have rounded to tenths of a percentage rather than to the closest whole percentage, given how small the percentages are). So, for example, 0.3% of 1H signs in ASL are swings (1 out of 367), and 0.8% of 2HIB signs in ASL are swings (3 out of 382), and 10.6% of 2HRM signs are swings (35 out of 331). (These percentages were calculated from table B.24. For the 2HRM figures we divided the swing column figure by the sum of the 2HRM, 2HRM swing, and 2HRM over time figures.)

TABLE 3.2. Swing Signs as Percentages of Noncurve Signs

	1H Swings	2HIB Swings	2HRM Swings
ASL	0.3%	0.8%	11.0%
BSL	0.7%	0.3%	12.2%
LIS	0.7%	0.6%	14.7%
LSF	2.6%	0	13.8%
Auslan	4.8%	0	18.3%

The almost complete absence of swing signs for 2HIB signs is due to the fact that the swinging is typically immediately above or below the base (as in MUSIC in ASL), so these signs are subsumed under the **OnB** set. Only Auslan and LSF make considerable use of swings in 1H signs (although Auslan's percentage is almost double that of LSF's). We note, without explanation, that these are the two languages that have no instances of 2HIB swings. But all the languages make considerable use of swings in 2HRM signs, and that is largely because all 2HR signs with inversion are, by definition, swing signs. Auslan, LSF, and LIS use 2HRM swing signs proportionately more than BSL and ASL.

Statistical Significance

Chi-square statistical analysis on the swing sign data set for 1H signs (contrasting the sum of swing signs to nonswing, noncurve signs) shows the languages to be extremely highly significantly different ($\chi^2 = 35.5$; ***$p < .0001$). Auslan and LSF approach statistically significant difference ($\chi^2 = 3.5$; $p = .06$), but since the chi-square value is not high, we ran a Fisher's exact test and found that Auslan and LSF show a significant difference on the left tail. Since the two tests show different results, we lack clarity. That is, Auslan appears to have a greater predominance of 1H swing signs than LSF. In sum, no firm clusterings were apparent for 1H swing signs.

It was not possible to perform a chi-square statistical analysis for 2HIB signs because the number of swing signs was too small.

Chi-square statistical analysis on the swing sign data set for 2HRM signs (contrasting the sum of swing signs to nonswing, noncurve signs) shows the languages to be significantly different again ($\chi^2 = 11.9$; *$p < .05$), and clusterings are apparent. So we ran additional tests. ASL, LIS, and LSF have a 35% chance of being the same ($\chi^2 = 2.1$). However, BSL and Auslan are statistically different ($\chi^2 = 7.0$; *$p < .05$). Auslan is the outlier here; it employs swings much more than the other languages. If we perform a chi-square statistical analysis on only the other four languages (just to demonstrate that Auslan really is the outlier), we find that they are not significantly different ($\chi^2 = 2.4$; $p = .49$). In sum, rather than showing any type of clustering, Auslan is simply different: it employs statistically significantly more 2HRM swing signs than the other languages.

The Goal with Respect to 2HRM Signs

From the data so far in this chapter on 2HRM noncurve signs, we see no obvious goal comparable to what we saw for 1H signs or 2HIB signs. That is, although the directions **Away, Down, Ipsil,** and combinations of any of these are much more common than the other directions, none of these directions stands out from the others as being the overwhelming goal and, further, none involves a tactile anchor.

It could be that 2HRM signs differ from the other two types precisely in the fact that they lack anything comparable to a goal. We doubt that, however. In chapter 5 we will look at two-handed reflexive signs in which the reflexivity is defined across some plane other than the Mid plane. We will see there a strong tendency for movement of the hands toward or (to a lesser extent) away from each other, that is, movement toward or away from the plane of symmetry. This finding seems natural to us. After all, the symmetry is defined across the plane, so the plane plays a definitional role in these signs. Nevertheless, the tendency with respect to the plane is both toward and away from it—so the goal, if you would, is bipolar in a sense.

If 2HRM signs had the same tendency, we would see a preponderance of signs that have the direction **Contral** (that is, toward the Mid plane) or any combination of **Contral,** or the direction **Ipsil** (that is, away from the Mid plane) or any combination of **Ipsil.** We must include 2HRM swing signs that are **Contral-Ipsil** or any combination of **Contral** on one phase of the swing and any combination of **Ipsil** on the other phase. When we look at such signs, we find the totals given in table 3.3, confirming exactly such a preponderance, where the last column gives the percentage of all 2HRM signs that involve **Contral** and/or **Ipsil.** Thus 2HRM signs do have a goal, after all—just a bipolar one.

TABLE 3.3. 2HRM Signs Involving Contral or Ipsil

	Nonswing	Swing: **Contral-Ipsil**		All Signs Involving **Contral** or **Ipsil**
	Contral	**Ipsil**		
ASL	51	78	0	41%
BSL	62	92	6	38%
LIS	49	65	13	48%
LSF	74	93	16	43%
Auslan	52	131	67	47%

Adaptive Modularity Hierarchy

We have returned to the notion of adaptive modularity repeatedly in this chapter's discussion of signs with noncurve paths. From this discussion emerges the adaptive modularity hierarchy.

Adaptive Modularity Hierarchy

For 1H:	**GOAL > Away > Down > Ipsil > Up > Contral > Rear**
For 2HIB:	**GOAL > Away > Ipsil > {Down, Up} > Rear > Contral**
For 2HRM:	**{Away, Down} > Contral > Up > Ipsil > Back**
Overall hierarchy:	**GOAL > Away > Down > Ipsil > Up > Contral > Rear > Back**

For 1H the GOAL is **Ts**; for 2HIB the GOAL subsumes **Tb + OnB + PastB.** The umbrella of GOAL in our hierarchy, then, actually includes many (combinations of) **Back** (for 1H signs) and (combinations of) **Contral** (for 2HIB signs) examples. So we expect that **Back** and **Contral** (as part of Goal) are actually of a higher adaptive modality than our Venn diagrams would lead one to believe. This hierarchy reflects the centrality of GOAL to primary movement.

Overview of Signs with Noncurve Paths

If we step back from the details of individual signs and look just at the three gross categories across the languages, an interesting observation jumps out. In table 3.4 we give the percentage of signs with a noncurve path, including swing signs, for 1H, 2HIB, and 2HRM with respect to the total number of signs with primary movement of all types in our data corpus. The high consistency of percentages across the languages for 1H signs ($\chi2 = 1.1$; $p = .90$) and the lack of significant difference for 2HRM signs ($\chi^2 = 8.9$; $p = .06$; although we are approaching significant difference here) contrasts sharply with the extremely highly significant differences in 2HIB signs ($\chi^2 = 55.7$; ***$p < .0001$). BSL and Auslan are strongly similar to one another in their prevalence of 2HIB signs ($\chi^2 = 0.4$; $p = .51$), but ASL exhibits a much higher percentage of 2HIB signs than LSF ($\chi^2 = 29.5$; ***$p < .0001$) and LIS ($\chi^2 = 42.9$; ***$p < .0001$). Indeed, when we compare only LSF and LIS, we find they are not statistically significantly different from each other ($\chi^2 = 3.3$; $p = .07$). ASL, it turns out, does not fit in either group nicely. When we group ASL with Auslan and BSL, we find a significant difference ($\chi^2 = 9.9$; *$p < .05$); likewise, when we group ASL with LIS and LSF we find an extremely highly significant difference ($\chi^2 = 52.2$; ***$p < .0001$). But the difference between ASL and BSL/Auslan is a whole power different from the difference between ASL and LIS/LSF.

Motivation for Aberrations within 2HIB Signs

Why should LIS and, to a lesser extent, LSF disfavor 2HIB signs so strongly? There are at least two possible lines of inquiry one could follow here. One is to look for the answer in the surrounding spoken

TABLE 3.4. Noncurve Signs as Percentage of All Signs

	1H	2 HIB	2HRM
	Signs	Signs	Signs
ASL	29%	30%	25%
BSL	30%	25%	28%
LIS	31%	18%	27%
LSF	30%	21%	30%
Auslan	30%	26%	28%

language culture to which these Deaf communities are exposed, in particular, at the gestures used by that culture. Hearing people use gestures as they speak (Kendon 1980, 1988; McNeill 1985, 1992; Kita 1993, 2000; Duncan 1996; Haviland 2000; LeBaron and Streeck 2000; Özyürek 2000; and so many others); in fact, some scholars have claimed all spoken languages are accompanied by gesture (Duncan 2002). Indeed, prohibiting speakers from gesturing during speech leads to changes in speech (Graham and Argyle 1975; Graham and Heywood 1975; Ríme et al. 1984; Ríme and Schiaratura 1991; Rauscher, Krauss, and Chen 1996), with adverse impact when the content expressed is spatial (Rauscher, Krauss, and Chen 1996).

Efron (1941) separated gestures used by hearing people into various groups, one of which he called "symbolic gestures," which can accompany speech but can also be used without speech to convey the same information. Ekman and Friesen (1969) redubbed these "emblems." Among gestures, emblems are the closest to signs (McNeill 2000a). Spoken Italian has been claimed to be rich in emblems, much richer than spoken British English (Kendon 1995; 2004a). Pika, Nicoladis, and Marentette (2006) label both spoken Italian and spoken French (and spoken Spanish—a point we will return to in chapter 7) high-frequency-gesture cultures in comparison with English, a low-frequency-gesture culture. (For more comments on these claims, see Iverson et al. 2008. Other languages claimed to belong to low-frequency-gesture cultures include Japanese [von Raffler-Engel 1980] and Chinese [Chen 1990].)

Although claims of this sort (particularly about Italian and other southern European languages) are not uncommon, as far as we know, they have not been supported by methodical empirical study. Indeed, papers in McNeill (2000b) and in Müller and Posner (2004), among others, argue that many types of gestures are frequent across all languages. And Gullberg (1998) found no difference in frequency of gestures between northern Europeans (Swedes) and southern Europeans (French). Still, the question of whether Italian and French speakers use emblems, in particular, more than English speakers do is open.

What we do know, however, is that both hearing and deaf people linguistically exploit visually motivated gestures. Such gestures can be used by hearing people to develop sign languages (Umiker-Sebeok and Sebeok 1987; Kendon 1988; Farnell 1995; Morford, Singleton, and Goldin-Meadow 1995; Kegl, Senghas, and Coppola 1999; Morford and Kegl 2000). Further, deaf people coin many signs from visually motivated gestures that become conventionalized (for ASL see Emmorey and Reilly 1995; Liddell 2003; for BSL see Sutton-Spence and Woll 1999; for LIS see Volterra and Erting 1990; for Auslan see Johnston and Schembri 2007; and see studies of home sign, such as Goldin-Meadow and Mylander 1990; Butcher, Mylander, and Goldin-Meadow 1991; Yau 1992; Singleton, Morford, and Goldin-Meadow 1993; Goldin-Meadow 2003).

None of this should be the least surprising. Approximately 96% of deaf children are born to hearing parents (Moores 2001). So many signs must, perforce, be created in the context of a hearing adult and a deaf child attempting to communicate. The presence of a gestural substrate to signs is, accordingly, inevitable.

Given all this, if it is, in fact, the case that spoken Italian and French are high-frequency-gesture cultures with respect to emblems and if, further, it is a fact that emblems are typically 1H or 2HRM but not typically 2HIB (something we have found no systematic studies of or claims about, but that appears to be true just from looking at studies of Neapolitan emblems in de Jorio 1832 and Kendon 2004a, 2004b), then it could very well be (and some would argue should be) that emblems in the spoken language influence the distribution of signs in the sign languages. Iverson et al. (2008) show that, whereas both Italian and American children use many gestures, Italian children use a wider range of emblems than American children do (where the latter confine themselves mostly to deictic gestures). As part of their conclusions, they say, "Exposure to a rich gestural model may attune Italian children to the ways in which representational information can be captured by the manual modality. . . ." (2008, 175). Deaf children are also exposed to these emblems, so it is not unreasonable to expect these emblems to have effects on deaf children's use of their hands in speech. The low incidence of 2HIB signs in LIS and, to a lesser extent, LSF, then, could be due to the influence of emblems in the spoken languages of Italian and French.

Another possible line of inquiry has to do not with influence from hearing culture but with influence from manual alphabets. Both BSL and Auslan use a two-handed manual alphabet, in contrast to the one-handed manual alphabet of the other three languages. Accordingly, they have a number of loan signs (that is, signs that grew out of fingerspelling; see Battison 1978) in which one hand moves while the other is immobile (Sutton-Spence, Woll, and Allsop 1990; Sutton-Spence and Woll 1993; Sutton-Spence 1998; Sutton-Spence and Woll 1999; Schembri and Johnston 2004, 2007; Johnston and Schembri 2007)—that is, 2HIB signs. In comparing loans in BSL (discussed in Brennan 2001) with loans in ASL (discussed in Brentari and Padden 2001) and LSQ (Quebec Sign Language; discussed in Miller 2001), Brentari asserts, ". . . the restructuring of borrowings reflects constraints on word formation in one- and in two-handed signs" (Brentari 2001, xvii) according to whether the language has a one-handed alphabet or a two-handed one. Additionally, compounds in BSL are influenced by the fact that it has a two-handed alphabet (Brennan 2001). Are these facts responsible for the relative dearth of 2HIB signs in LIS and LSF in contrast to BSL and Auslan? A careful examination of our corpora is needed before we can answer this. This approach nicely separates out ASL from BSL and Auslan, since ASL has a one-handed manual alphabet very similar to LSF's and LIS's. On the other hand, the fact remains that ASL is much more different from LSF and LIS than it is from BSL and Auslan—a random result if the manual alphabet is the true explanation for the division.

One more remark is in order, though, before we leave this issue behind. If it can be shown that ASL makes use of initialized signs more frequently than does either LSF or LIS to the same (or nearly same) extent that ASL uses 2HIB signs more frequently than does either LSF or LIS, it is possible that this frequency difference in initialization accounts for the disparate prevalence of 2HIB signs that we have observed here. We know of no study that compares the frequency of initialization among these three languages, unfortunately. However, we have doubts about this possibility. First, although ASL had an explosive expansion of initialized signs in the 1970s (Supalla 2004), a wide range of initialized signs in ASL today are quite old and, significantly for us, based on the French word (having entered ASL from LSF) rather than the English word (see passing comments in the literature, including Bornstein 1990, 93; Baker-Shenk and Cokely 1991, 460; among many others), so that today they are not even recognizable as having had their origins in initialization (such as the C-handshape of LOOK-FOR from French *chercher*, the A-handshape of WITH from French *avec*, the V-handshape of STUPID (made at the forehead) from French *vide*, and so on). So Old LSF certainly made significant use of initialization. Second, the high incidence of initialization in LSQ has been attributed to contact with LSF (Machabée and Dubuisson 1995). Third, Mexican Sign Language, which also stems at least partially from LSF, has a much higher incidence of initialization than ASL (Faurot et al. 1999). We suspect, then, that LSF makes significant use of initialization. Further, Yau (1990, 273) suggests that initialization happens "under the influence of phonetic writing systems" and that of the three spoken languages, English, French, and Italian, Italian has the closest match between alphabetic letter and sound segment; so we do not expect LIS to shun initializations.

Clearly this is an area for further study.

Comparison of Directions across the Three Types of Signs

With respect to the original claim we encountered that started our study—the claim that BSL uses the direction **Away** (or combinations involving **Away**) more heavily than ASL does and that ASL uses the direction **Back** (or combinations involving **Back**) more heavily than BSL does—we offer figures that compile noncurve signs of all types in our study. First, let's consider the usage percentage comparison of (combinations of) **Away** across all noncurve signs in these five languages, as in figure 3.21. Despite the subjective impression that BSL makes the greatest use of (combinations of) **Away** and that ASL makes the least, the data supporting this are not statistically significant. These findings suggest that the subjective impression of signers that BSL uses (combinations of) **Away** more heavily than ASL is restricted to certain sign types.

Our data disconfirm the claim that ASL uses (combinations of) **Back** more heavily than BSL. Indeed, the languages vary very little with respect to how heavily they use (combinations of) **Back,** as seen in figure 3.22. In making figure 3.22, for 1H and 2HIB signs we analyzed the direction **Ts** as a complex of **Back.** As a way of comparing the languages for (combinations of) **Back** usage, this is valid. However, note that the very fact that in this study we did not break down **Ts** signs into components (for example, **BackDown** or **BackUp**) means that information from **Ts** signs is missing from our

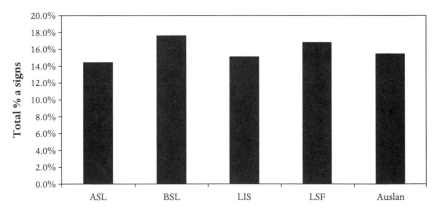

Figure 3.21. Comparison of Overall **Away** Proportions in Noncurve Signs
($\chi^2 = 7.8; p > .10$)

ANALYSIS OF SIGNS WITH NONCURVE PATHS

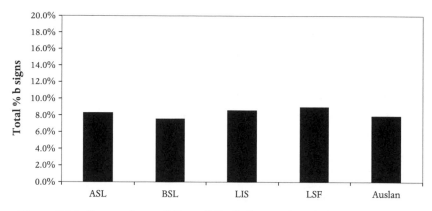

Figure 3.22. Comparison of Overall **Back** Proportions in Noncurve Signs
($\chi^2 = 2.7; p = .60$)

later figures on overall proportions of signs using (combinations of) **Ipsil, Down,** and **Up.** So although it gives valid comparative information across languages, figure 3.22 is not to be used to compare against figures 3.23 through 3.25.

We made similar comparisons for **Ipsil, Up,** and **Down.** Note that we could not include **Contral** in these comparisons, since **Contral** was not isolated in our 2HIB signs (but is, instead, subsumed under **Tb** and under some, but not all, of the **OnB** and **PastB** signs).

The resulting information for **Ipsil** is given in figure 3.23. This time the spread is almost five points, with LIS using (combinations of) **Ipsil** the most and BSL using (combinations of) **Ipsil** the least. The effect is that LIS uses the lateral extremities of the signing space more than BSL does. One could say that the signer is more expansive in LIS than in BSL.

This fact is interesting. A possible explanation, again, is influence from gestures that accompany speech: speakers of Italian (and of French) tend to use bigger gestures (gestures that take up more space) than speakers of many other languages (Gullberg 1998; Cienki and Müller 2008). We further note a mild genetic split here, with BSL and Auslan being on the less expansive side and the others being on the more expansive side.

ANALYSIS OF SIGNS WITH NONCURVE PATHS

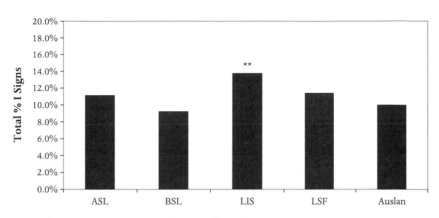

Figure 3.23. Comparison of Overall **Ipsil** Proportions in Noncurve Signs
($\chi^2 = 16.5$; **$p < .005$)

An alternative explanation for the less expansive signing space of BSL and Auslan in contrast to the other languages, and a more promising one, lies in the two-handed fingerspelling system. That is, the ongoing need to fingerspell may be a force toward keeping the hands in proximity to each other in these languages. But in the other three languages, with a one-handed alphabet, no such force would be operative. With a one-handed fingerspelling system, the signer can fingerspell in a wide range of spatial locations while simultaneously articulating signs with the other hand, such as classifier expressions. There has been no specific study of the prevalence of fingerspelling in BSL to our knowledge, but it has been estimated that conversational BSL contains approximately 10% fingerspelling (Deuchar 1978; Sutton-Spence 1994; although Brennan 2001 suggests that figure is too high but does not offer an alternative) and the same figure came up in a study of Auslan (Schembri and Johnston 2007, 332); these figures are certainly high enough to make such an account plausible.

The results for **Up** (in figure 3.24) and **Down** (in figure 3.25), however, did not offer interesting generalizations (although we do note that Auslan and ASL contrast with the other three languages in figure 3.25, a grouping we have not seen elsewhere). Although the differences for **Down** are statistically significant, the spread is less than 3%, a difference that we cannot claim to be noticeable to a signer.

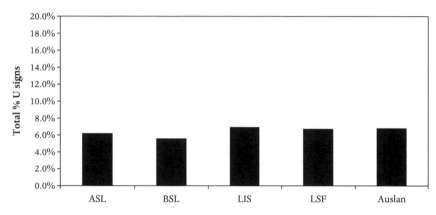

Figure 3.24. Comparison of Overall **Up** Proportions in Noncurve Signs
($\chi 2 = 3.4; p = .49$)

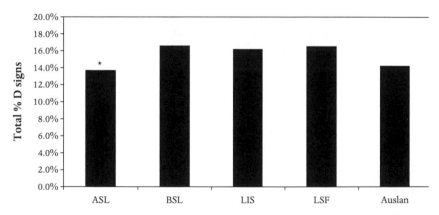

Figure 3.25. Comparison of Overall **Down** Proportions in Noncurve Signs
($\chi^2 = 9.9; ^\star p < .05$)

4

Analysis of Signs with Curve Paths in ASL, BSL, LIS, LSF, and Auslan

The raw data that form the basis for the Venn diagrams, charts, and statistics in this chapter are presented in the tables in appendix C.

General Remarks on Analyses

We organized the signs with curve paths according to whether the movement was CW or CCW as seen on the HZ, VW, or Mid plane. We determined CW versus CCW on the Mid plane by looking at the hands from the right side of the signer; we made that determination on the HZ plane by looking down at the hands from above (even if the sign was made above the signer's eye level); we made that determination on the VW plane by looking at the hands from the signer's point of view.

With respect to 2HRM signs, notice that the plane the curve is defined on is independent of the plane of symmetry.

One-Handed Curve Signs (1H)

With regard to 1H signs the relative sums for the various types of curves in each direction are given in figure 4.1. In illustrations 4.1 through 4.3, we see 1H curve signs in ASL in which the curve is visible on the Mid plane, the HZ plane, and the VW plane.

ANALYSIS OF SIGNS WITH CURVE PATHS

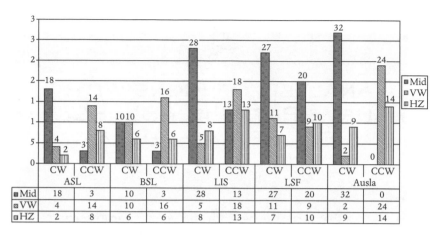

	CW	CCW	CW	CCW	CW	CCW	CW	CCW	CW	CCW
	ASL		BSL		LIS		LSF		Ausla	
▣ Mid	18	3	10	3	28	13	27	20	32	0
▨ VW	4	14	10	16	5	18	11	9	2	24
▥ HZ	2	8	6	6	8	13	7	10	9	14

Figure 4.1. 1H Curve Signs across the Five Languages

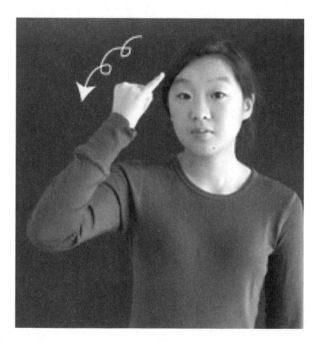

Illustration 4.1. PARANOID in ASL, Example of 1H Curve Sign
Visible on Mid Plane

Illustration 4.2. LOTS-TO-DO in ASL, Example of 1H Curve Sign
Visible on HZ Plane

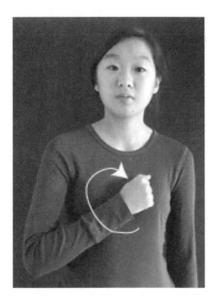

Illustration 4.3. SORRY in ASL, Example of 1H Curve Sign Visible
on VW Plane

ANALYSIS OF SIGNS WITH CURVE PATHS

When curves are visible on the Mid plane, all languages favor CW. The preference is clearest in Auslan, where we found no CCW curves visible on the Mid plane. When curves are seen on the HZ plane, instead there is a preference for CCW, except in BSL, where there is no preference either way. Likewise, when curves are seen on the VW plane, there is a preference for CCW (and, again, Auslan's preference is so strong, only one sign was CW out of a total of nineteen), except in LSF, where there is a small preference for CW. Thus the plane of the curve is the determining factor on direction, rather than the language.

Two-Handed Curve Signs in Which One Hand Is an Immobile Base (2HIB)

With regard to 2HIB signs, the relative sums for the various types of curves in each direction are given in figure 4.2. In illustrations 4.4 through 4.6, we see 2HIB curve signs in ASL in which the curve is visible on the Mid plane, the HZ plane, and the VW plane.

Again, for curves visible on the Mid plane, CW direction is favored even more strongly than with 1H signs. With curves seen on the other two planes, however, the languages differ. For curves

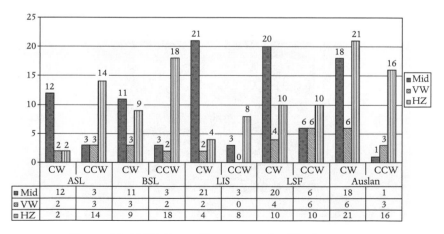

	CW	CCW	CW	CCW	CW	CCW	CW	CCW	CW	CCW
	ASL		BSL		LIS		LSF		Auslan	
■ Mid	12	3	11	3	21	3	20	6	18	1
▨ VW	2	3	3	2	2	0	4	6	6	3
▥ HZ	2	14	9	18	4	8	10	10	21	16

Figure 4.2. 2HIB Curve Signs across the Five Languages

ANALYSIS OF SIGNS WITH CURVE PATHS

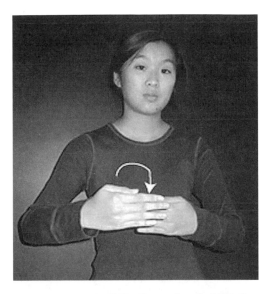

Illustration 4.4. AFTER in ASL, Example of 2HIB Curve Sign
Visible on Mid Plane

Illustration 4.5. CHOCOLATE in ASL, Example of 2HIB Curve
Sign Visible on HZ Plane

Illustration 4.6. ENGAGED in ASL, Example of 2HIB Curve Sign
Visible on VW Plane

visible on the HZ plane, ASL, BSL, and LIS favor the CCW direction, but LSF shows no preference and Auslan shows a slight preference for CW. And for curves visible on the VW plane, ASL and Auslan strongly favor CCW, whereas LSF slightly favors it, and BSL and LIS favor CW.

Two-Handed Curve Signs with Reflexive Symmetry across the Midsaggital Plane (2HRM)

With regard to 2HRM signs, the relative sums for the various types of curves in each direction are given in figure 4.3. In illustrations 4.7 through 4.9, we see 2HRM curve signs in ASL in which the curve is visible on the Mid plane, the HZ plane, and the VW plane.

ANALYSIS OF SIGNS WITH CURVE PATHS

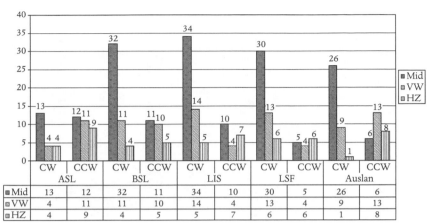

	CW	CCW	CW	CCW	CW	CCW	CW	CCW	CW	CCW
	ASL		BSL		LIS		LSF		Auslan	
Mid	13	12	32	11	34	10	30	5	26	6
VW	4	11	11	10	14	4	13	4	9	13
HZ	4	9	4	5	5	7	6	6	1	8

Figure 4.3. 2HRM Curve Signs across the Five Languages

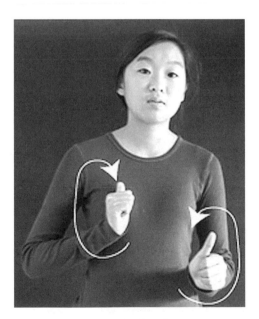

Illustration 4.7. ACT in ASL, Example of 2HRM Curve Sign Visible on Mid Plane

ANALYSIS OF SIGNS WITH CURVE PATHS

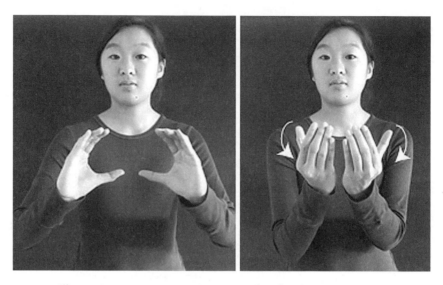

Illustration 4.8. CLASS in ASL, Example of 2HRM Curve Sign
Visible on HZ Plane

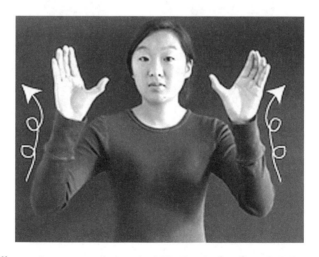

Illustration 4.9. DECORATE in ASL, Example of 2HRM Curve
Sign Visible on VW Plane

As expected by now, curves seen on the Mid plane strongly favor a CW direction across the languages, with the surprise that the preference is only slight in ASL. Also as expected, 2HRM curves seen on the HZ plane favor the CCW direction across the languages, with the exception that LSF shows no preference and with the caveat that the overall preference is slight. Auslan, again, is the most extreme. But when we turn to 2HRM curves seen on the VW plane, the preference is by language. ASL and Auslan favor CCW, LIS and LSF strongly favor CW, and BSL slightly favors CW.

Overview of Curve Signs

Amassing the curve data for each language in figures 4.4 through 4.8, certain trends become apparent.

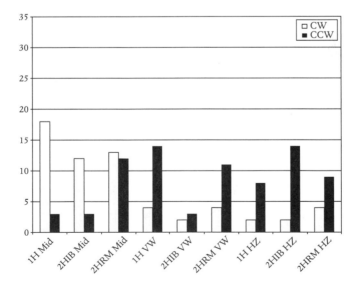

Figure 4.4. ASL Curve Signs

ANALYSIS OF SIGNS WITH CURVE PATHS

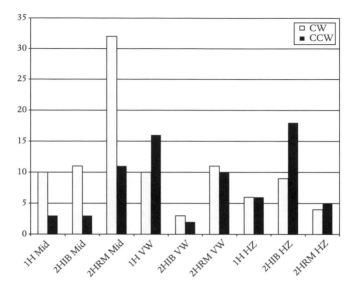

Figure 4.5. BSL Curve Signs

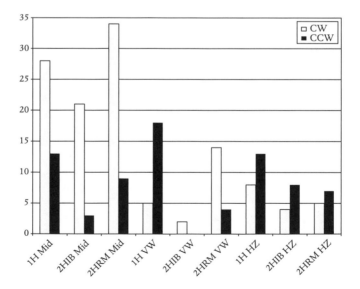

Figure 4.6. LIS Curve Signs

ANALYSIS OF SIGNS WITH CURVE PATHS

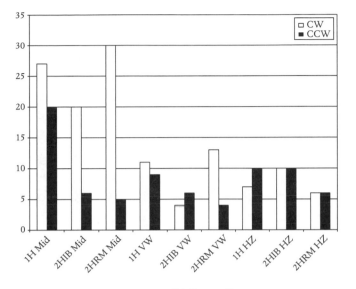

Figure 4.7. LSF Curve Signs

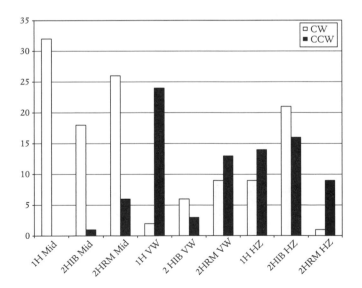

Figure 4.8. Auslan Curve Signs

All the languages favor CW movement when the curve is visible on the Mid plane, with BSL consistently showing three to one favor across the three types of signs, but the other languages showing very strong favor to only slight favor depending on the type of sign.

But when it comes to curves visible on the HZ plane, four of the languages favor CCW movement across the three types of signs, with the exception that BSL shows no favor on 1H and that LSF shows no favor on 2HIB. How strong the favor is varies by language across the three types of signs. Auslan stands apart from the other languages, however, in favoring CCW for 1H and 2HRM but CW for 2HIB.

Likewise, when it comes to curves visible on the VW plane, four of the languages go one way and one is an outlier. But this time four of the languages are mixed, varying between CW and CCW across the three types of signs with no single thread in common. ASL, however, favors CCW consistently, although the favor is least strong for 2HIB.

In sum, we see no trends along genetic lines. Nor do we see trends along origin-bound versus diaspora lines.

Just as we did with signs that have noncurve paths, we now step back from the details of individual signs and look only at the gross categories across the languages, given in table 4.1.

Curve signs in ASL and BSL are more common with 2H reflexive signs (lumping all the planes the curves are visible in), whereas curve signs are more common in LIS, LSF, and Auslan with 1H. However, these clusters are not statistically significant.

TABLE 4.1. Percentage Curve Signs for Each Sign Type on Each Plane

	1H	2HIB	2HRM M	2HRM VM	2HRM HZ
ASL	34%	25%	36%		5%
BSL	30%	27%	42%		2%
LIS	43%	19%	37%		2%
LSF	40%	27%	32%		1%
Auslan	37%	30%	29%	0.5%	3%

TABLE 4.2. Curve Sign Summary

	Curves
ASL	11%
BSL	11%
LIS	21%
LSF	15%
Auslan	12%

If, next, we look at the total number of curve signs as a percentage of the overall signs (in table 4.2), an interesting fact emerges. LIS exploits signs with a curve path to a much greater extent than the other languages. Indeed, a high percentage of curve path signs could be said to be a distinguishing characteristic of LIS in contrast to the other languages here.

Statistical Significance

1H Curve Signs

Chi-square statistical analysis comparing the prevalence of 1H curve signs across the languages reveals an extremely highly significant difference among them ($\chi^2 = 43.9$; ***$p < .0001$). Further testing shows that BSL and Auslan have an 11% chance (that is, more than double what would be needed to establish a significant difference, but certainly not a huge chance) of being the same ($\chi^2 = 2.5$; $p = .11$); however, the members of the other genetic family do not cluster together. Instead, a comparison of ASL, LIS, and LSF again reveals an extremely highly significant difference among them ($\chi^2 = 22.0$; ***$p = .0001$).

When it comes to comparing the prevalence of 1H curve signs in which the curve is visible on the Mid plane versus being visible on the other planes, we find that the languages show a statistically significant difference ($\chi^2 = 13.3$; *$p < .05$). Further tests showed that the languages split here along genetic lines. ASL, LIS, and LSF had a 28% chance of being the same ($\chi^2 = 2.6$; $p = .28$), whereas BSL and Auslan had but a 10% chance of being the same ($\chi^2 = 2.7$; $p = .10$).

The diaspora languages also clustered together, even more strongly, with ASL, LIS, and Auslan showing a rather forceful 51% chance of being the same ($\chi^2 = 1.3; p = .51$). But the origin-bound languages were highly statistically different here ($\chi^2 = 11.9; **p < .005$).

When it comes to comparing the prevalence of 1H curve signs in which the curve is visible on the VW plane versus being visible on the other planes, we find that the languages again show a statistically significant difference ($\chi^2 = 12.3; *p < .05$). Further tests revealed that the genetic family of ASL, LIS, and LSF have a 31% chance of being the same ($\chi^2 = 2.4; p = .31$). However, BSL and Auslan were statistically significantly different here ($\chi^2 = 4.7; *p < .05$). When we, instead, tested for an origin-bound versus diaspora clustering, we found that ASL, LIS, and Auslan had a 54% chance of being the same ($\chi^2 = 1.2; p = .54$), but BSL and LSF were highly significantly different ($\chi^2 = 10.4; **p < .005$).

In sum, with respect to which plane a curve is visible in for 1H curve signs, the diaspora languages cluster together strongly, whereas the origin-bound languages are significantly different from each other, and the LSF family of signs clusters together relatively strongly, whereas the BSL family of signs shows either very slight clustering or significant differences.

With respect to whether the direction of movement is CW or CCW, however, the languages have a whopping 96% chance of being the same when it comes to 1H curve signs ($\chi^2 = 0.6; p = .96$).

2HIB Curve Signs

Chi-square statistical analysis comparing the prevalence of 2HIB curve signs across the languages reveals a highly significant difference among them ($\chi^2 = 20.3; **p < .005$). Once more, further testing shows that BSL and Auslan have a 66% chance of being the same ($\chi^2 = 0.2; p = .66$); however, the members of the other genetic family do not cluster together. Instead, a comparison of ASL, LIS, and LSF again reveals a highly significant difference among them ($\chi^2 = 17.4; **p < .005$). The outlier here is ASL. If we remove the

ASL data and compare just LIS and LSF, we find they show a 36% chance of being the same ($\chi^2 = 0.8$; $p = .36$).

With regard to removing ASL from the data pool here, please recall our discussion of robust statistics in chapter 3. There we explain that we followed the practice of first comparing data on the whole group, then removing outliers that are manually (or visually) easy to detect—so easy that we could have removed them from the start; that is, their outlier status does not emerge from the statistical comparisons but simply from screening the raw data. In this way, we are staying in line with the prescribed methods of robust analysis.

When we ran tests comparing the prevalence of 2HIB signs with a curve visible on the Mid plane versus all other planes, we found a significant difference among the languages ($\chi^2 = 9.6$; *$p < .05$). Further tests showed a genetic split. ASL, LIS, and LSF have a respectable 49% chance of being the same ($\chi^2 = 1.4$; $p = .49$) and BSL and Auslan have a whopping 89% chance of being the same ($\chi^2 = 0.02$; $p = .89$). When it came to testing for a split along diaspora versus origin-bound lines, however, the diaspora languages were significantly different ($\chi^2 = 6.7$; *$p < .05$), whereas the origin-bound languages showed only a 10% chance of being the same ($\chi^2 = 2.7$; $p = .10$).

When we ran tests comparing the prevalence of 2HIB signs with a curve visible on the HZ plane versus all other planes, we found a significant difference among the languages ($\chi^2 = 11.7$; *$p < .05$). Further testing revealed a genetic split. ASL, LIS, and LSF have a 50% chance of being the same ($\chi^2 = 1.4$; $p = .50$), whereas BSL and Auslan have an 85% chance of being the same ($\chi^2 = 0.04$; $p = .85$). So the genetic split is strong. There was no clustering of diaspora ($\chi^2 = 6.3$; *$p < .05$) versus origin-bound ($\chi^2 = 5.4$; *$p < .05$) languages, however.

Tests comparing the prevalence of 2HIB signs with a curve visible on the VW plane versus all other planes revealed a 48% chance of the languages being the same ($\chi^2 = 3.5$; $p = .48$).

With respect to whether the direction of movement is CW or CCW, we see a marked difference from what we saw with 1H curve signs. For 2HIB curve signs the languages are significantly different ($\chi^2 = 9.8$; *$p < .05$). There is no genetic split here: BSL and Auslan are significantly different ($\chi^2 = 4.2$; *$p < .05$) and ASL, LIS, and LSF have only a 6% chance of being the same ($\chi^2 = 5.5$; $p = .06$). The diaspora languages are significantly different from one another ($\chi^2 = 7.5$; *$p < .05$). The origin-bound languages, however, do cluster together, with a 28% chance of being the same ($\chi^2 = 1.2$; $p = .28$).

2HRM Curve Signs

Finally, chi-square statistical analysis comparing the prevalence of 2HRM curve signs across the languages reveals an extremely highly significant difference among them ($\chi^2 = 31.4$; ***$p < .0001$). Yet again, further testing shows that BSL and Auslan have a slight, 6% chance of being the same ($\chi^2 = 3.4$; $p = .06$); however, the members of the other genetic family still show an extremely highly significant difference among them ($\chi^2 = 19.1$; ***$p < .0001$). This time the outlier is LIS. If we remove the LIS data and compare just ASL and LSF, we find they have an 83% chance of being the same ($\chi^2 = 0.05$; $p = .83$).

When we ran tests comparing the prevalence of 2HRM signs with a curve visible on the Mid plane versus all other planes, we found the languages to have a 62% chance of being the same ($\chi^2 = 2.6$; $p = .62$). Tests comparing the prevalence of 2HRM signs with a curve visible on the HZ plane versus all other planes revealed the languages to have a 54% chance of being the same ($\chi^2 = 3.1$; $p = .54$). Tests comparing the prevalence of 2HRM signs with a curve visible on the VW plane versus all other planes showed the strongest similarity: the languages have a 77% chance of being the same ($\chi^2 = 1.8$; $p = .77$).

With respect to whether the direction of movement is CW or CCW, we see a highly significant difference among the languages ($\chi^2 = 16.6$; **$p < .005$). The genetic family of BSL and Auslan shows a 28% chance of being the same ($\chi^2 = 1.2$; $p = .28$). But ASL, LIS, and LSF are highly significantly different ($\chi^2 = 15.5$; **$p < .005$). When looking for a diaspora versus origin-bound split, we found the origin-bound languages of BSL and LSF to have a 50% chance of being the same ($\chi^2 = 0.5$; $p = .50$), but the diaspora languages were highly significantly different ($\chi^2 = 12.3$; **$p < .005$). In fact, however, the ASL data obscure an important fact. If we remove the ASL data, we find that the other four languages have a 22% chance of being the same ($\chi^2 = 4.4$; $p = .22$).

Summary of Statistics

Statistically, then, the diaspora versus origin-bound clustering is not strong with respect to curve signs. However, the genetic clustering is.

BSL and Auslan are not significantly different when it comes to the prevalence of curve paths across the three different types of signs studied here. They also are not statistically significantly different with respect to 2HRM curve signs—considering both the plane the curve is visible in and the direction of the movement path. For 1H curve signs they are significantly different only with respect to signs in which the curve is visible on the VW plane. For 2HIB curve signs they are significantly different only with respect to the direction of the movement path. Overall, BSL and Auslan are very much alike when it comes to curve signs.

ASL, LIS, and LSF are not statistically significantly different with respect to 1H and 2HIB curve signs—considering both the plane the curve is visible in and the direction of the movement path. And for 2HRM curve signs they are not significantly different except with respect to the direction of movement.

However, LIS shows a unique strong tendency: it favors curve signs, extremely so for 1H and 2HRM signs, as compared with the other languages.

5

UNUSUAL SYMMETRY OR OTHER ODDITIES IN ASL, BSL, LIS, LSF, AND AUSLAN

Some two-handed signs exhibit a variety of interesting complexities regarding symmetry. Where symmetry is defined over time, all such signs involve reflexivity across the Mid plane. The raw data are found at the end of appendix B. Where reflexive symmetry is defined across a plane other than the Mid plane or where symmetry is rotational or translational, the raw data are found in appendix D. Additional characteristics of primary path movement are also discussed in this chapter.

Reflexive Symmetry over Time

All reflexive symmetry over time in all five languages is exhibited only with respect to the Mid plane. There are two types.

One type involves both hands moving on the ipsilateral side and then on the contralateral side (ChSi = changing sides). Within that type, there are two further possibilities. First, you could move both hands in the same way, as though you were doing a 2HRM sign first with the Mid plane rotated 45° to the right, then with it rotated 45° to the left (ChSi 2HRM), as in PANTS in ASL, seen in illustration 5.1. Second, you could move only one hand with the other as an immobile base (ChSi 2HIB), as in JESUS in ASL, seen in illustration 5.2.

Another type involves doing something with one hand, then doing it with the other (Alt = alternating). An example is BOX (the fighting action, not the container), as shown in illustration 5.3. This is by far the most common type (fifty-six out of a total of eighty-seven in these five languages). Within this type you could

UNUSUAL SYMMETRY OR OTHER ODDITIES

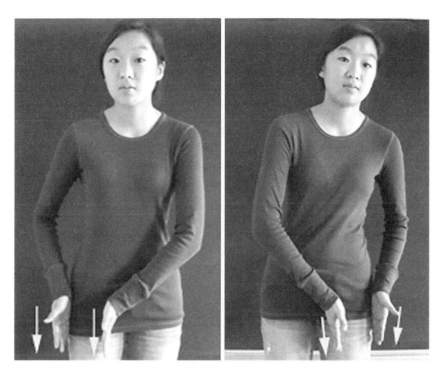

Illustration 5.1. PANTS in ASL, Example of ChSi 2HRM Sign

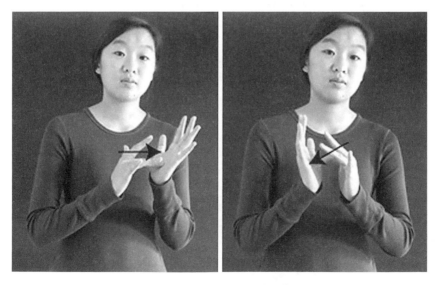

Illustration 5.2. JESUS in ASL, Example of ChSi 2HIB Sign

UNUSUAL SYMMETRY OR OTHER ODDITIES

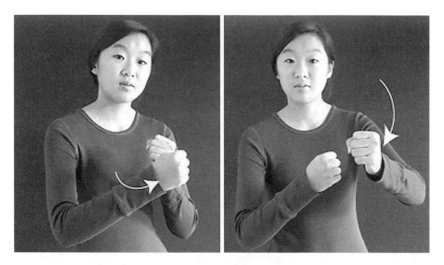

Illustration 5.3. BOX in ASL, Example of Alt 1H Sign

move the hands in the reflexive position directly across the plane from each other (Alt 1H), or you could glide each time, so that one hand is higher/lower or more forward/backward than the other (Alt 1H glide). An example of Alt 1H glide is the ASL sign STAIRS, in which one hand establishes a level, then the other hand establishes a level a little higher, and so on, seen in illustration 5.4.

All five languages exhibit all four subtypes with the one exception that LIS has no Alt 1H signs in our database. However, we know from other sources that LIS does, indeed, have such signs and we

Illustration 5.4. STAIRS in ASL, an Example of Alt 1H Glide Sign

note that our LIS database, although substantial, is the smallest of our corpora for these five languages.

Something interesting emerges from analyzing these signs. In ASL and LIS these signs have either two time points or an indefinite number of time points. But in LSF, BSL, and Auslan, the ChSi signs have exactly two time points and the alternating signs (Alt 1H and Alt 1H glide) have precisely two, three, or four time points, respectively. The dictionaries were quite clear on that. There are two exceptions. In Auslan one ChSi 2HRM sign is marked for four time points, and in LSF one Alt 1H glide sign can be done an indefinite number of times. The precision of time points makes these three languages stand apart from the others. It appears that losing precise time points, as ASL and LIS may have done, is the more innovative characteristic.

Chi-square statistical analysis of the data on reflexive symmetry over time in the five languages approaches statistical significance ($\chi^2 = 8.8$; $p = .067$). For the sake of future investigations and research, let's look at what these data might tell us, despite the lack of statistical significance. Excluding the origin-bound languages from the chi-square analysis, the statistical significance of the data decreases drastically ($\chi^2 = 0.8$; $p = .67$), suggesting that the diaspora languages cluster. Inclusion of only the origin-bound languages reveals a similar trend ($\chi^2 = 0.5$; $p = .50$), suggesting that the origin-bound languages cluster as well. Although these analyses tentatively indicate that the languages do indeed differ from one another and happen to split along origin-bound/diaspora lines, note that the data on reflexive symmetry over time account for at most only 2% of the data in any of these five languages.

Reflexive Symmetry across Planes Other Than the Midsaggital

Reflexive symmetry is found not just across the Mid plane but also across the HZ and the VW planes and across semantically selected planes.

Reflexive Symmetry across the Horizontal Plane (2HRHZ)

All five languages allow two-handed noncurve signs with reflexive symmetry across the HZ plane (2HRHZ; see illustration 5.5). Of the thirty-one total such signs, fourteen move either **Down** (eight) or **Up** (six), that is, movement is either toward the plane or away from it. So 2HRHZ signs show the same tendency for direction to be most affected by the anchor (or goal) plane as 2HRM signs show. ASL has six signs; BSL, six; LIS, two; LSF, seven; and Auslan, ten.

All these languages also allow 2HRHZ curve signs. Of the twenty-three total such signs, all have curves visible in the HZ plane only, and eleven of these have the dominant hand moving CW. All CW curves exhibit inversion, whereas only seven of the CCW ones do. BSL and LIS group together here in having no CW curves in our corpora.

We need to make one additional note here. According to our dictionaries, LIS stands alone in having signs in which the dominant

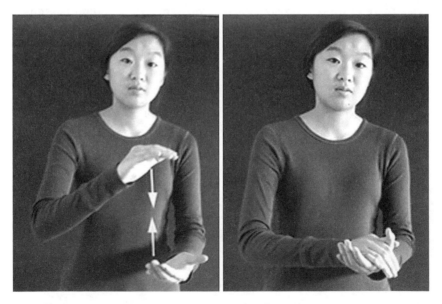

Illustration 5.5. MARRY in ASL, Example of 2HRHZ Noncurve Sign

UNUSUAL SYMMETRY OR OTHER ODDITIES

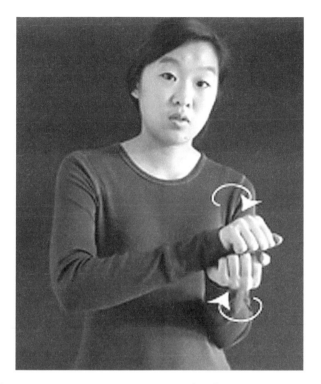

Illustration 5.6. CHEW in ASL, Example of 2HRHZ Curve Sign

(top) hand moves CCW while the bottom hand moves CW (e.g., TURNO 'turn' and MISTO 'mix'). Such a difference between the hands is not at all problematic when the movement is secondary, involving only wrist rotation, for example, as in wringing out a wet cloth or trying to open a jar. And we see that exact movement in various signs, including the ASL sign LAUNDRY. However, with respect to primary movement, it is exceptionally challenging to motor coordination. To see this, hold the hands reflexively symmetrical across any of the three relevant planes, then let the hands move in circles (where the elbows will also be moving, since this is primary movement). It is easy to keep them both going CW or CCW, with or without inversion. However, having either one go CW while the other goes CCW is as hard for us as tapping the head with one hand while rubbing a circle on the belly with the other. Therefore, even though this mismatch of movement nicely correlates to the meaning of the signs (dealing with mixing), we were doubtful. Upon consultation with two LIS signers (Simona Sportoletti and Rita Sala, personal communication, May 2009), we concluded that the dictionary arrows are regrettably inaccurate and that what we really have here is movement in a single direction by both hands, but with inversion.

Considering curve and noncurve signs, we see in table 5.1 that ASL makes more use of the HZ plane for symmetrical signs than the other languages, with Auslan not far behind. Chi-square statistical analysis reveals a 41% chance that the languages are the same ($\chi^2 = 4.0$; $p = .41$).

Reflexive Symmetry across the Vertical Wall Plane (2HRVW)

In our corpora all the languages except LIS have two-handed noncurve signs with reflexive symmetry across the VW plane (2HRVW), as seen in illustration 5.7. There are only eleven such signs in total, and fully five of them are found in our ASL database. Auslan also has one 2HRVW curve sign, CW seen on the VW plane. Chi-square statistical analysis reveals an 11% chance that the languages are the same ($\chi^2 = 7.6$; $p = .11$).

Reflexive Symmetry across a Semantically Selected Plane

All five languages allow symmetry across semantically selected planes (such as the plane that cuts through the ipsilateral shoulder used for certain signs about time and responsibility, or the plane that

TABLE 5.1. Percentage of 2HRHZ Signs across the Five Languages

	2HRHZ
ASL	1.1%
BSL	0.6%
LIS	0.5%
LSF	0.6%
Auslan	0.9%

UNUSUAL SYMMETRY OR OTHER ODDITIES

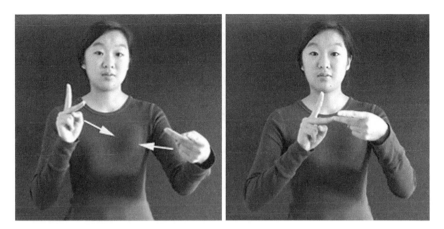

Illustration 5.7. PERFECT in ASL, Example of 2HRVW Noncurve Sign

cuts through the heart used for certain signs about love). In ASL we found thirteen (one of which has no primary movement); BSL, four; LIS, one; LSF, six (one without primary movement that is also a glide); and Auslan, nine (one without primary movement).

In all there are thirty-three such signs, with ASL showing the greatest use of them and LIS showing the least. We have no statistics to report here since it is not possible to perform a chi-square statistical analysis on data with fewer than five values.

Conclusions about These Unusual Reflexive Symmetries

With so few data, conclusions are elusive. However, ASL stands out as being the most active in using unusual reflexive symmetries.

Rotational Symmetry (2H-Rot)

All five languages exhibit two-handed rotational symmetry (2H-rot) signs distributed close to evenly across all three planes (fifteen each for Mid and HZ, and twelve for VW), as shown in table 5.2. An ASL example across the HZ plane is given in illustration 5.8. None of the languages exploit rotational symmetry much, but ASL does it twice as much as some and three times as much as others.

TABLE 5.2. Percentage of 2H-Rot Signs across the Five Languages

	2H-Rot Signs
ASL	1.2%
BSL	0.6%
LIS	0.5%
LSF	0.3%
Auslan	0.4%

Chi-square statistical analysis reveals a significant difference in the prevalence of rotational symmetries in the languages here ($\chi^2 = 12.2$; $^\star p < .05$). ASL is clearly the outlier. If we remove the ASL data, the other four languages have a 69% chance of being the same ($\chi^2 = 1.5$; $p = .69$).

Translation Symmetry (2H-Trans)

All five languages exhibit signs in which the hands have the same handshape and do the same movement, but not reflexively across

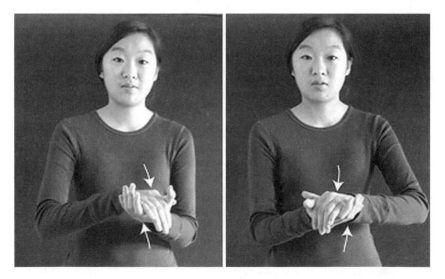

Illustration 5.8. HAMBURGER in ASL, Example of 2H-Rot Sign

a fixed plane or rotationally around a fixed axis. We label these "translation symmetries" (2H-trans). Many such signs are swings. The only 2H-trans swing path that would not tax motor coordination is **Contral-Ipsil**, and, indeed, all five languages avail themselves of such swings. ASL, however, makes much more use of swing translations than the other languages, as shown in table 5.3. An example is given in illustration 5.9.

All languages also have noncurve translations that are not swings. Some went only **Ipsil** or only **Contral**. For translations going **Away**, the path shapes were parallel waves or zigzags—with ASL and LSF not showing any in our corpora. For translations going **Down**, a wavy path appears in both ASL and BSL—with LIS and LSF not showing any **Down** translations in our corpora. An ASL example is given in illustration 5.10. BSL and Auslan also have translation signs in which the orientation of the palms distinguishes these signs from reflexive signs—going **Down** in both languages and **Up**, as well, for Auslan. We note that when orientation is the distinguishing factor of a translation, the hands are connected. Given the high number of 2HRM signs with connected hands in ASL (mentioned in the next section) and the even higher number of giant-hand signs in ASL (mentioned in chapter 2 in the section "Signs That Do Not Fit into Our Analyses," where the hands are connected by definition), we find it interesting that Auslan exploits connecting the two hands in forming translation signs to increase the number of directions those hands can go, whereas ASL does not.

TABLE 5.3. Percentage of 2H-Trans Swing Signs across the Five Languages

	2H-Trans Swing
ASL	1.1%
BSL	0.3%
LIS	0.4%
LSF	0.1%
Auslan	0.2%

UNUSUAL SYMMETRY OR OTHER ODDITIES

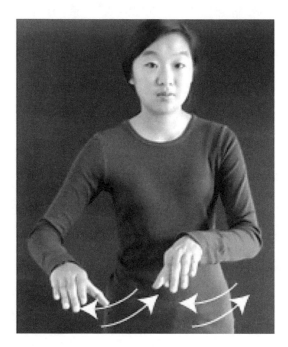

Illustration 5.9. ACTIVITY in ASL, Example of 2H-Trans Swing Sign

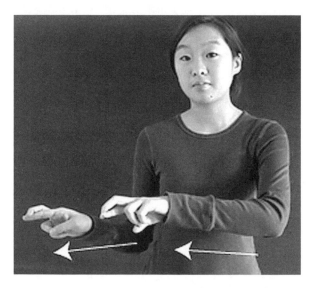

Illustration 5.10. READY in ASL, Example of 2H-Trans Nonswing Sign

UNUSUAL SYMMETRY OR OTHER ODDITIES

TABLE 5.4. Percentage of 2H-Trans Noncurve Signs (Minus Swings) across the Five Languages

	2H-Trans Noncurve, Nonswing
ASL	0.6%
BSL	0.7%
LIS	0.6%
LSF	0.9%
Auslan	0.9%

We see in table 5.4 that none of the languages seems to make considerably more use of these signs than the others.

When we turned to curve paths, we found that none of the languages shows many translations. Still the data reveal something interesting. LIS has none in our corpora. Auslan (with eight) and ASL (with nine) limit theirs to curves visible on the HZ plane only, with Auslan always connecting those hands (making moot any issue of motor coordination). BSL (with nine) and LSF (with three), however, allow translation curves visible on both the HZ and VW planes. An example of an ASL 2H-trans curve sign is shown in illustration 5.11.

When we sum all the different types of 2H-trans signs, as in table 5.5, we find that ASL is exploiting them considerably more than the other languages. The number of 2H-trans signs in ASL is somewhat surprising, given that Frishberg (1975) noted that iconic translations tend to yield to reflexive symmetries in the history of ASL.

Chi-square statistical analysis reveals a 7% chance that the languages are the same with respect to use of 2H-trans ($\chi^2 = 8.8$; $p = .07$).

Overview of Unusual Symmetries

In table 5.6 we give the sum of all the unusual symmetries we found in our corpora. Chi-square statistical analysis shows that the languages are highly significantly different when we compare the

Illustration 5.11. TORNADO in ASL, Example of 2H-Trans Curve Sign

TABLE 5.5. Percentage of 2H-Trans Signs across the Five Languages

	2H-Trans
ASL	2.4%
BSL	1.7%
LIS	1.0%
LSF	1.2%
Auslan	1.4%

prevalence of unusual symmetries in the whole data corpus from each language ($\chi^2 = 17.9$; **$p < .005$). We found that by removing the ASL data, chi-square statistical analysis showed a 12% chance that the remaining four languages are the same ($\chi^2 = 5.8$; $p = .12$). So ASL truly stands out as the heaviest user of unusual symmetries.

Other Movement Characteristics That May Help to Distinguish between Languages

BSL and Auslan exhibited movements on a few signs that were unlike anything found in our dictionaries of ASL, LIS, and LSF.

UNUSUAL SYMMETRY OR OTHER ODDITIES

TABLE 5.6. Summary of Symmetries Other Than Plain 2HRM

	Ref Sym over Time	Ref Sym VW	Ref Sym HZ	Sym Rotation	Sym Trans	Unusual Symmetries
ASL	13	5	14	16	31	6.1%
BSL	23	2	9	9	25	4.5%
LIS	6	0	5	5	10	2.7%
LSF	26	3	9	5	18	4.2%
Auslan	19	1	16+1	7	27+1	3.8%

First, in our corpora BSL has one sign that involves movement of the bent dominant arm only—a flapping, as of a wing: SCOTLAND (mimicking playing the bagpipes). Auslan has three flapping wing signs and a fourth sign in which the "wing" draws a CCW circle seen on the HZ plane. None of the other language dictionaries included so-called wing signs. However, when we turned to our analysis of ISN (discussed in chapter 7), we did find one wing sign there: GALLINA 'hen'. This is a polysyllabic sign in which the dominant hand does secondary movement at the nose, then both "wings" flap; it is also clearly iconic.

Second, for a handful of signs our dictionaries of BSL and Auslan indicate head tilts, shoulder shrugs, torso leans, jaw droppings, and body twists—something the other dictionaries do not indicate in lexical items, in contrast to small movements such as nose wrinkling and eyebrow raises, which dictionaries in all five languages noted. We have not considered movement of the nonmanuals in this study, but if the dictionaries are representative (that is, if this is not simply some difference in lexicographical work), only BSL and Auslan use these larger nonmanuals on lexical items in a robust way, whereas all five use these larger nonmanuals for syntactic purposes (as far as we could tell from brief and sometimes scattered remarks in the dictionaries). We note that, although research on nonmanuals is more prevalent in recent years, this fact cannot account for the difference in our findings, since the BSL dictionary we are using is the oldest in our corpus.

Again, however, we must add that when we turned to our ISN data (which we discuss in chapter 7), we found many signs in which the head, in particular, made large, highly noticeable movements. One iconic one was BAUTISMO 'baptism', in which the dominant hand holds the nose closed while the head dips forward then backward dramatically. Since the movement of the hand follows perforce from the movement of the head, we categorized this sign as involving no primary movement. Another iconic one is CANTAR 'sing', in which the dominant hand stays immobile in front of the mouth, like a handheld microphone, while the head tilts side to side. Again, no primary movement is involved, so we do not include this sign in our analysis. Given that at a young stage of ASL much information now carried by the hands was carried by the nonmanuals (Frishberg 1975), one might speculate that such work by the nonmanuals is typical of young sign languages (see Yau 2008); but that account certainly does not extend to BSL and Auslan.

Additionally, in 2HRM signs, sometimes the hands distinctly cross the plane (not just come to the plane, with perhaps the fingertips extended over). With respect to noncurve paths, this happens in fifteen signs in ASL, nine in BSL, four in LIS, nine in LSF, and fifteen in Auslan. It also happened in two curve paths in Auslan, in one 2H-trans in LIS, and in two **Contral-Ipsil** swings in LSF. The percentages are shown in table 5.7, and an example from ASL is given in illustration 5.12. Although there is a fairly continuous spread, ASL makes the most use of crossing the plane. However, the difference is not statistically significant. Chi-square statistical analysis of these crossing signs as a percentage of all signs shows the languages to have a 38% chance of being the same ($\chi^2 2 = 4.2$; $p = .38$). And chi-square analysis of the 2HRM signs that cross the plane as a percentage of 2HRM signs shows the languages to have a 19% chance of being the same ($\chi^2 = 6.1$; $p = .19$).

UNUSUAL SYMMETRY OR OTHER ODDITIES

TABLE 5.7. Percentage of 2H Symmetrical Signs in Which the Hands Cross the Midsaggital Plane

	2H Signs, Hands Cross Midsaggital, % of All Signs	2HRM Signs, Hands Cross Midsaggital, % of 2HRM Signs
ASL	1.2%	5.0%
BSL	0.6%	2.0%
LIS	0.5%	2.0%
LSF	0.8%	2.0%
Auslan	0.9%	3.0%

Also in 2HRM signs we noted that many have the hands connected. For noncurve paths ASL has twenty-two; BSL, thirty-one; LIS, twelve; LSF, seventeen; Auslan, thirty-eight. For curve paths LIS has one; LSF, three; Auslan, two. In other symmetries, we find that ASL has connected hands on three translation signs. BSL has connected hands on one 2HR across a semantically defined plane, on thirteen translation signs, and on three candidates for polysyllabic signs. LIS has connected hands on one 2HRHZ sign and on five translation signs. LSF has connected hands on four translation signs. Auslan has connected hands on sixteen translation signs. The totals and relevant percentages (among the total number of primary movement signs) are seen in table 5.8, and an example from ASL is shown in illustration 5.13.

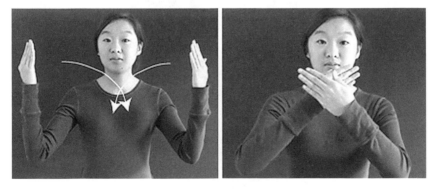

Illustration 5.12. DARK in ASL, Example of 2HRM with Hands Crossing the Plane

TABLE 5.8. 2H Symmetrical Signs in Which the Hands Are Connected

	2H Signs, Hands Connected
ASL	2%
BSL	3%
LIS	2%
LSF	2%
Auslan	3%

Although the differences are not great, we see that BSL and Auslan make more use of connected hands than the other languages. In fact, chi-square statistical analysis reveals a significant difference among the languages ($\chi^2 = 11.9$; $^\star p < .05$). When we perform additional chi-square tests, we do, indeed, find a genetic split; ASL, LIS, and LSF have an 81% chance of being the same ($\chi^2 = 0.4$; $p = .81$), whereas BSL and Auslan have a 71% chance of being the same ($\chi^2 = 0.1$; $p = .71$). However, when we test for a split along the diaspora/origin-bound line, we find that the diaspora languages (ASL, LIS, and Auslan) have only a 10% chance of being the same ($\chi^2 = 4.6$; $p = .10$), whereas the origin-bound languages (BSL and LSF) are statistically significantly different ($\chi^2 = 7.3$; $^\star p < .05$).

Illustration 5.13. GO-BY-BOAT in ASL, Example of 2HRM Sign with Hands Connected

6

RESULTS FROM THE STUDY OF ASL, BSL, LIS, LSF, AND AUSLAN

In this chapter, we give the generalizations we have found that hold across the five languages examined thus far and the implications of these generalizations. We then summarize the findings on particular languages and on clusterings of languages. Based on the analyses of the data in chapters 3 through 5, we offer testable hypotheses about sign languages in general, which we then put to the test in chapter 7.

Generalizations across All Five Languages

Adaptive Modularity

The uniformity of adaptive modularity of path directions for 1H noncurve signs across the languages is striking. The distribution of overlapping path directions for 2HRM signs is less uniform but still very similar across the languages. Overall adaptive modularity is lower for most directions with 2HIB noncurve signs than it is with 1H noncurve signs and with 2HRM noncurve signs. We repeat the hierarchy here:

Adaptive Modularity Hierarchy

For 1H:	GOAL > **Away** > **Down** > **Ipsil** > **Up** > **Contral** > **Rear**
For 2HIB:	GOAL > **Away** > **Ipsil** > {**Down, Up**} > **Rear** > **Contral**
For 2HRM:	{**Away, Down**} > **Contral** > **Up** > **Ipsil** > **Back**
Overall hierarchy:	GOAL > **Away** > **Down** > **Ipsil** > **Up** > **Contral** > **Rear** > **Back**

108

(Recall that **Back** is absent from the 1H hierarchy since **Back** signs were subsumed under **Ts**. Likewise most **Contral** signs are absent from the 2HIB hierarchy since they were subsumed under the combination of **Tb**, **OnB**, and **PastB**.)

Although we initially approached the whole issue of prevalence of directions within the framework of trying to find ways to typologize languages, the finding that a hierarchy exists and that it is so consistent across the languages is potentially of serious importance to sign phonetics. Degrees of adaptive modularity may give insight into what combinations of direction movements are physiologically possible for signs with noncurve paths. One might then be able to make a model of a possible unmarked phonetics regarding movement directions for a sign language and measure deviations from this norm. We leave this as a suggestion for future research.

Anchors/Goals

Signs favor movement toward an anchor or goal. For 1H signs, the goal is the signer. For 2HIB signs, the goal is the base hand. For 2H signs that involve reflexive symmetry across a plane (regardless of which plane), the goal (which is bipolar) is the plane of symmetry.

In chapter 3 we suggested that tactile feedback could be a factor in accounting for the existence of goals in 1H and 2HIB signs. However, for 2H signs that involve reflexive symmetry the goal does not offer tactile feedback. Nevertheless, it is possible that a common motivation is at play in goal selection for all these types of signs, a motivation that is physiological.

A physician's checkup sometimes includes nonequilibrium tests for motor coordination. Among these tests (Shumway-Cook and Woollacott 2007, 118) are the following:

1. Finger to nose. The shoulder is abducted to 90°, with the elbow extended. The patient is asked to bring the tip of the index finger to the tip of the nose. Alterations may be made in the initial starting position to assess performance from different planes of motion.

2. Finger to therapist's finger. The patient and therapist sit opposite each other. The therapist's finger is held in front of the patient. The patient is asked to touch the tip of the finger to the therapist's index finger. The position of the therapist's finger may be altered during testing to assess ability to change distance, direction, and force of movement.
3. Finger to finger. Both shoulders are abducted to 90° with the elbows extended. The patient is asked to bring both hands toward the midline and approximate the index fingers from opposing hands.

Being able to bring the fingertip to the nose is a basic motor ability, as is being able to bring it to the therapist's hand and to the fingertip of the opposing hand precisely at the Mid plane. These are things the ordinary healthy person can do; they do not strain our eye-hand coordination. Notice that each of these three tests could be seen as a canonical test for exactly the motor coordination needed in reaching the goal in 1H, 2HIB, and 2HRM signs, respectively. That is, reaching a part of the self that does not migrate on its own (the nose), reaching an object that can migrate (the hand of the therapist in the case of the motor test, and of the signer in the case of articulating 2HIB signs), and coordinating the hands to meet at a plane midway between them—these are what most signs ask the signer to be able to do, and these are things that most healthy people should be able to do.

It appears that the movements that are unmarked with regard to motor coordination (that is, movements toward the goal) are the movements that are more prevalent than any other type. Since language is a participatory activity that healthy people should be able to join in on, this correlation makes perfect sense. We therefore suspect that all sign languages will not only have goals for the three types of signs but also precisely the same goals that the five languages studied here have. We formalize this in the anchor principle.

> **Anchor Principle:** Signs favor movement toward an anchor or goal. For 1H signs, the goal is the signer. For 2HIB signs, the goal is the

base hand. For 2H signs that involve reflexive symmetry across a plane (regardless of which plane), the goal (which is bipolar) is the plane of symmetry.

Curve Path Signs

Our observations fall into two groups, one concerning the plane in which the curve is visible and the other concerning the direction (CW or CCW) of the curve.

Plane of Curve Visibility for Reflexive Signs

When symmetry is defined across a plane other than the Mid plane, only curves visible in the plane of symmetry are found. So, in our corpora all five languages allow 2HRHZ curve signs, with the curve visible only in the HZ plane. Only Auslan allows 2HRVW curve signs; it has a single such sign with the curve visible in the VW plane.

Most symmetry, of course, is defined across the Mid plane, and this is where we find variation on what plane the curve is visible in.

These findings have an immediate explanation in the notion of markedness (just as we suspect above with respect to goals). The Mid plane is the unmarked plane for signs exhibiting reflexive symmetry; there are multiple times more 2HRM signs than 2HRHZ or 2HRVW signs. In the marked situations (that is, when reflexivity is defined relative to any plane other than the Mid plane), the curve is restricted to being visible in the plane of symmetry. In this way, the curve adds no further complications to an already marked sign. We formulate this as a markedness constraint.

> **Curve Markedness Constraint:** If the plane of symmetry for a curve sign is marked, then the curve must be visible in the plane of symmetry.

Direction of the Curve

With respect to 1H curve signs, when curves are visible on the Mid plane, all languages favor CW. Indeed, statistically the languages have a 96% chance of being the same ($\chi^2 = 0.6$; $p = .96$). When curves are seen on the HZ plane, there is a preference for CCW, except in BSL, where there is no preference either way. When curves are seen on the VW plane, there is a preference for CCW, except in LSF, where there is a small preference for CW. Thus for 1H signs the plane of the curve is the determining factor on direction, rather than the language. We have no account of these facts. The data just sit there and stare at us.

For 2HIB and 2HRM signs, the situation is more complex. When the curve is visible on the Mid plane, all the languages favor CW movement.

When the curve is visible on the HZ plane, three of the languages favor CCW movement, whereas LSF shows no favor one way or the other, and Auslan favors CCW for 2HRM signs but CW for 2HIB signs.

When the curve is visible on the VW plane, the data defy our attempts at generalizations. BSL and LIS favor CW direction, ASL favors CCW, LSF favors CCW for 2HIB signs but CW for 2HRM signs, and Auslan does just the opposite of LSF.

We hesitate to draw conclusions from such unruly data, although we note that the most unruliness occurs when the curve is visible on the VW plane, which is the plane where the direction of movement is most immediately apparent to both the signer and the person being signed to. Maybe the fact that the VW plane allows such easy visibility of the path direction licenses more play here.

Characteristics by Which One Language Stands apart from the Others

Here we list many characteristics that set a single language off from the other languages in a statistically significant way or for which the differences are readily apparent from the Venn diagrams.

Other statistically significant differences were found in our data, all with respect to noncurve path signs and the percentage differences between uses of directions that are polar opposites of each other. For example, with respect to 2HRM noncurve signs, in Auslan **Ipsil** is favored over **Contral** (where **Ipsil** and **Contral** are polar opposites of each other) to a higher degree than in the other languages; in fact, the difference is highly significant. Yet we are skeptical of calling this a linguistic property. Rather, it seems to be a mathematical artifact of manipulating the data and is not part of the visual phonetics of the languages. We have, therefore, not included these findings in this chapter. However, all the data are included in earlier chapters for future researchers.

We remind the reader, however, of additional differences between the languages noted throughout the book. For example, in chapter 2 there are comments about the relative prevalence of fixed location/referent signs (which are rare in ASL) and giant-hand signs (which are disproportionately many in ASL).

In chapter 3, we point out differences across the languages between the adaptive modularity of various directions of movement for the three major types of signs. For example, in ASL **Contral** has very low to no adaptive modularity in 1H noncurve signs. For 2HIB noncurve signs LIS stands out as having the strongest preference for **Tb** over **OnB**, whereas Auslan stands out as making almost as great use of **OnB** as **Tb** and as wildly favoring **OnB** over **PastB**.

These other characteristics might well be quite telling in trying to recognize a given sign language, perhaps as telling as the differences we list now.

Characteristics of ASL:

1. ASL allows less combining of directions in 2HIB signs than the other languages do.
2. ASL exploits unusual symmetries (i.e., reflexivity over time; reflexivity across the HZ plane, the VW plane, and semantically selected planes; rotational; and translation) significantly more than the other languages do.

Characteristics of LIS:

1. LIS 2HIB noncurve signs make greater use of **Up** than the other languages.
2. LIS 2HRM noncurve signs favor **Down** more than the other languages.
3. LIS exploits signs with a curve path more than the other languages, with a statistically significant difference when it comes to 2HRM signs.
4. LIS has no 2HRVW noncurve signs.

Characteristics of Auslan:

1. Auslan 2HIB signs allow the most combining of directions in comparison with 2HIB signs in the other languages.
2. Auslan employs 2HRM swings significantly more than the other languages.
3. Auslan uses swings in 1H signs heavily.

The lack of statistically significant characteristics for only LSF and for only BSL could be telling. That these two languages have not developed new characteristics setting them uniquely apart from the other languages may lend further support to our proposal that origin-bound languages behave differently from diaspora languages.

Characteristics That Languages Cluster Around

Here we list many characteristics that set clusters of languages off from the other languages in a statistically significant way or for which the differences are readily apparent from the Venn diagrams, and we discuss their implications.

Again, other statistically significant differences were found in our data, all with respect to noncurve path signs and the percentage differences between uses of directions that are polar opposites of each other. For example, with respect to 1H noncurve signs, in ASL and LIS **Ipsil** is favored over **Contral** (where **Ipsil** and **Contral** are polar opposites of each other) to a higher degree than in the other languages; in fact, the difference is highly significant. Our same skepticism rises; this looks like a mathematical artifact rather than a part of the visual phonetics of the languages. We have therefore not included these findings in this chapter. However, all the data are included in earlier chapters for future researchers.

Again, we remind the reader of additional differences languages cluster around that have been noted throughout the book. For example, chapter 2 mentions the relative prevalence of elbow signs in ASL and LIS that involve primary movement, as compared with the other languages, which use mostly only secondary movement with elbow signs. Chapter 5 discusses the fact that for 2HRM over time signs, BSL, Auslan, and LSF have a precise number of times the sign repeats, but ASL and LIS do not. Chapter 5 also mentions that only Auslan and BSL have wing signs (with a nod to a single wing sign in ISN, studied in chapter 7). These two languages also use large nonmanuals (torso tilts, head nods, and the like) in more robust ways in the lexicon than the other languages (again, with a nod to several such signs in ISN). (And we cautioned that this finding could be the result of differences in lexicographical work.)

Characteristics Distinguishing Genetic Families

We found the greatest coincidence of language characteristics among genetically related languages. Here is the list:

1. The languages differ statistically significantly with respect to **Ipsil** for 1H noncurve signs, with the BSL family using **Ipsil** much less frequently than the LSF family. Further tests show an 80% certainty that BSL and Auslan are the same ($\chi^2 = 0.1$; $p = .80$), whereas a comparison of ASL, LIS, and LSF shows a 77% certainty that the three languages are the same ($\chi^2 = 0.5$; $p = .77$).
2. The geography of 2HIB signs with respect to adaptive modularity splits on genetic lines quite neatly.
3. When we combine **Tb, PastB,** and **OnB** 2HIB noncurve signs into one group called "base signs," the languages cluster on genetic lines, with the BSL family having a significantly higher prevalence of base signs than the LSF family.

4. With 2HRM signs, for **Contral** there is a significant contrast ($\chi^2 =$ 13.4; $^*p < .05$), with the LSF family using **Contral** much more than the BSL family. The LSF, LIS, and ASL family exhibits a 59% chance of being the same ($\chi^2 = 1.1$), and the BSL and Auslan family exhibits a 46% chance of being the same ($\chi^2 = 4.0$).

5. BSL and Auslan make significantly more use of connected hands in two-handed symmetrical signs (including all types of symmetries) than the other three languages. BSL and Auslan have a 71% chance of being the same ($\chi^2 = 0.1$; $p = .71$), whereas ASL, LIS, and LSF have an 81% chance of being the same ($\chi^2 = 0.4$; $p = .81$).

From this list, we note that significant differences are found in all three major types of signs: 1H (in one), 2HIB (in two and three), and 2HRM (included in four and five). So the genetic split is profound.

Another conclusion can follow when we combine this list with information in chapter 3. We note that although prevalence of base signs (that is, 2HIB signs that are **Tb, OnB,** or **PastB**) is genetically determined (in three), how the languages actually utilize the base is not. Indeed, there are highly significant differences across the languages when we split these signs up into the three groups of **Tb** ($\chi^2 = 18.5$; $^{**}p < .005$), **OnB** ($\chi^2 = 50.2$; $^{**}p < .005$), and **PastB** ($\chi^2 = 16.9$; $^{**}p < .005$). No patterns emerge; it simply looks as if each language does its own thing. For example, in all the languages **Tb** is larger than **OnB**, but in Auslan it is larger only by 6%, whereas in LIS it is larger by 300%. Additionally, **OnB** is larger than **PastB** in all the languages, but in LIS and LSF the difference is relatively small, whereas in all the other languages **OnB** is a minimum four times greater than **PastB**, and in Auslan it is ten times greater. We conclude from this that although gross characteristics may be genetic, finer distinctions can reveal a wide range of innovations that cross genetic lines.

One final word. Although there are no other characteristics for which the languages neatly split into these particular two clusters, there are characteristics for which one genetic family adheres but the other does not. For example, BSL and Auslan were alike on prevalence of 1H curves, but the other languages did not cluster together. But with respect to which plane a curve is visible in for 1H curve signs, the LSF family of signs clusters together relatively strongly, whereas the BSL family either shows very slight clustering or significant differences. Additionally, our statistics show that BSL and Auslan are almost identical in their prevalence of 2HIB curves and 2HRM curves. But the LSF family is not coherent; LIS and LSF are similar with respect to 2HIB, leaving ASL the outlier, and ASL and LSF are similar on 2HRM signs, leaving LIS the outlier. So there is surely some genetic clustering going on with respect to curve signs. And, finally, LIS and LSF cluster on one characteristic, but the other three languages do not: with 2HIB signs LSF and LIS only mildly favor **OnB** over **PastB,** whereas ASL and Auslan hugely favor **OnB** over **PastB,** and BSL strongly does so.

Likewise, the relative consistency of percentages across the languages for 1H and 2HRM signs contrasts sharply with the differences in 2HIB signs. BSL and Auslan are strongly similar to one another in 2HIB signs, but ASL exhibits a much higher percentage of 2HIB signs than LSF and, especially, LIS.

We are, therefore, led to a summary proposal that makes no distinction between noncurve and curve signs:

> **Genetic Permeation:** Genetic differences will permeate all three major types of signs.

Characteristics Distinguishing Origin-Bound from Diaspora Languages

We also found that the (creolized or hybridized or externally influenced) daughters of a mother language that had changed location (from France to Italy or to the United States; from Great Britain to Australia), that is, the diaspora languages, had characteristics that separated them from the daughters that remained in the homeland, which we call the "origin-bound languages." We list these:

1. The languages differ statistically significantly with respect to **Away** for 1H noncurve signs; BSL and LSF use **Away** much

more prevalently than the others do. Further tests show a 75% certainty that BSL and LSF are the same ($\chi^2 = 0.1$; $p = .75$), whereas a comparison of ASL, LSF, and LIS shows an 82% certainty that the three languages are the same ($\chi^2 = 0.4$; $p = .82$).

2. The languages differ statistically significantly with respect to **Down** for 1H noncurve signs; BSL and LSF use **Down** more prevalently than the others. Further tests show a 14% certainty that BSL and LSF are the same ($\chi^2 = 2.2$; $p = .14$), whereas a comparison of ASL, Auslan, and LIS shows a 64% certainty that the three languages are the same ($\chi^2 = 0.9$; $p = .64$).

3. In terms of the overall geography of the intersections of path directions for 1H noncurve signs, BSL and LSF are the most similar to each other, the only difference being in the relative size of the various intersections; ASL and LIS are also very similar to each other, with Auslan more closely resembling ASL and LIS with respect to combinability than BSL and LSF.

Looking at the first characteristic, and being influenced by the great degree of coherence (75% on one group and 82% on the other), we are led to a tentative proposal (in which the term "origin-bound daughters" indicates daughters that remain in the geographical home of the mother language and do not experience great contact with other sign languages):

Origin-Bound Favors Away: Origin-bound daughters will make greater use of **Away** in 1H signs than diaspora daughters.

On the assumption that characteristics shared by origin-bound daughters have been in the languages longer (perhaps since the start), this proposal suggests that sign languages start out using **Away** heavily. So we are led to another tentative proposal:

Young Favors Away: Young sign languages will make heavy use of **Away** in 1H signs.

All these proposals (as well as the anchor principle and the curve markedness constraint) can be tested. Testing genetic permeation, of course, calls for a study of genetically related languages.

The proposals Origin-bound Favors **Away** and Young Favors **Away**, however, can be testing by looking at other origin-bound languages and other young languages.

Analogous proposals could be made regarding the use of **Down** in 1H noncurve signs. We hesitate to do this, however, since the statistical difference regarding the use of **Down** among the languages, although significant, was not as convincing as that with **Away**.

Let us take a step back now and try to view these two characteristics together—the ones captured in Origin-bound Favors **Away** and Young Favors **Away**—and add to them the fact that we shied away from making a similar proposal regarding **Down**. Interestingly, the significant differences here all concern 1H noncurve signs. So the origin-bound versus diaspora split is not as profound as the genetic split seen above, which permeates all three types of signs. We find three things happening: the direction **Away** becomes less prevalent in the diaspora daughters, the direction **Down** becomes less prevalent in the diaspora daughters, and the adaptive modularity of the various directions goes up in the diaspora daughters. These findings are not unrelated. Basically, the diaspora daughters are making more use of more (combinations of) directions than the origin-bound daughters; they are innovative in this way.

That innovation should be seen most clearly with 1H signs is not surprising. The articulating hand in a 1H sign has a lot of freedom in what it can do (see Mai 2009 for discussion of an analogous point for secondary movement) so the diaspora languages are simply exercising that freedom. But in 2HIB signs, the articulating hand must relate closely to the base hand—so direction is automatically restricted. And in 2HR signs, the hand distinctly crossing the plane of symmetry (as opposed to simply coming to the plane or slightly crossing it) is disfavored. So once more, freedom of direction is hindered. Therefore the diaspora languages are innovating regarding primary path movement in the most likely type of signs to allow such innovation (1H), and the innovation itself is merely exploiting path directions to a fuller extent.

Again, a final word. Although there are no other characteristics for which the languages neatly split into these particular two clusters, there are characteristics for which the diaspora languages adhere but the origin-bound languages do not. For example, with respect to which plane a curve is visible in for 1H curve signs, the diaspora languages cluster together strongly, whereas the origin-bound languages are significantly different from each other.

Characteristics Distinguished by Contact Spoken Language

We also found a clustering that is neither along genetic lines nor along innovative/origin-bound lines. BSL, Auslan, and ASL form one cluster and LIS and LSF form another cluster on the following characteristic (which is now the first item on our new list of characteristics distinguished by contact spoken language):

1. With 2HIB noncurve signs, LIS and LSF make significantly more use of **Ipsil** than the other three languages.

But this is not the whole story. We found that BSL and Auslan had a much higher prevalence of 2HIB signs than LSF and LIS. So the languages clustered genetically, with ASL floating, in a sense. That is, ASL was statistically significantly different from BSL and Auslan, on the one hand, and extremely highly statistically significantly different from LSF and LIS, on the other ($***p < .0001$). Elsewhere we have not seen four of the languages forming two clusters with one language being aberrant. So this very situation itself is aberrant. Since ASL is 2 powers of 10 closer to the BSL-Auslan cluster than to the LSF-LIS cluster, and since it is clear that ASL has a high prevalence of 2HIB signs (even higher than BSL and Auslan do), whereas LIS and LSF disfavor these signs, we believe it would be a mistake not to include this information in our final picture of how the languages fall together. So we include the following characteristic, which is the second item on our list of characteristics distinguished by contact spoken language:

2. BSL and Auslan are almost identical to one another in the geography of 2HIB noncurve signs and in the extent to which they make use of these signs. ASL makes even higher use of these signs. LSF and, especially, LIS make lower use of these signs.

We find confirmation of our decision to include the above characteristic in the fact that once more we see a particular area for the clusterings: the significant differences here all concern 2HIB non-curve signs. We already discussed earlier (in chapter 3) the possibility of influence from gesture use in the contact spoken languages and the possibility of a two-handed versus one-handed alphabet being a factor here (the latter possibility being less likely, we believe, given that ASL, which has a one-handed alphabet, patterns with BSL and Auslan, which have a two-handed alphabet).

Characteristics Revealing Other Clusterings

There is one more clear clustering that is neither along genetic lines nor along diaspora/origin-bound lines. Here Auslan joins BSL and LIS, in contrast to ASL and LSF. (So we find a list with only one characteristic this time.)

1. For 2HIB noncurve signs, with respect to **Down**, ASL and LSF have a 77% chance of being the same ($\chi^2 = 0.1$), whereas LIS, BSL, and Auslan pattern together (with LIS using **Down** the least).

We note further that with 2H curves seen on the VW plane, both BSL and LIS favor CW direction, whereas the other languages either go CCW or go one way for 2HIB and the other for 2HRM. Additionally, for 2HRHZ curve signs, BSL and LIS allow only CCW, whereas ASL and LSF allow both and Auslan allows only CW. Since in both instances the other three languages do not cluster together, we merely mention these facts for the sake of completeness.

Overview of How the Languages Cluster on These Characteristics

If we simply add up the distinguishing characteristics for clusterings so far, we get a total of eleven. The table below shows the percentage similarity of each pair of languages with respect to the eleven specific characteristics outlined above. It does not reflect on overall similarity between languages nor even on lexical similarity. Further, we have not weighted the characteristics. That is, we judged the languages to be alike on each particular characteristic (assigning it value 1) or different (assigning it value 0). In using a toggle switch like this, we have wiped out the nuances the statistical data provide us—the nuances that allowed us to come up with this list of characteristics in the first place. The results are, thus, no longer quantitative, but purely qualitative. Finally, we choose to include only those eleven characteristics for which the differences between the languages are statistically significant or are obvious from the Venn diagrams or tables. We do not include data that fall outside these standards, many of which are, nonetheless, noticeable—such as the fact that Auslan and BSL have wing signs and the other languages do not. Indeed, seeing a wing sign for the first time can be disconcerting for a signer whose language does not include them; they are highly noticeable. The choice of imposing these standards on which characteristics we include and which we exclude in the table below influences the outcome perforce.

Different standards for inclusion of characteristics would result in different values in the cells of table 6.1. With this understanding in mind, we forge ahead to see what information we can find on the extent to which each pairing of languages shares the given characteristics of the movement parameter. According to our study, with respect only to those characteristics of the parameter of primary movement examined here and found to be statistically significant or obvious from our Venn diagrams and tables, a hierarchy can be made, with pairs higher up more similar to each other than pairs lower down:

Similarity Hierarchy
Auslan and BSL / LIS and ASL
LIS and LSF
LSF and ASL

RESULTS FROM THE STUDY

Auslan and ASL
Auslan and LIS
BSL and LSF
BSL and ASL
LIS and BSL
LSF and Auslan

The finding that the genetic sisters Auslan and BSL are very much alike is no surprise. In fact, Auslan and BSL are mutually comprehensible sign languages—essentially dialects of a single language. However, the fact that the genetic sisters LIS and ASL are as much alike with respect to these eleven characteristics as Auslan and BSL may come as a surprise, and perhaps a dismaying one to some. Certainly LIS and ASL are not dialects of a single language.

It is standard among lexicographers of spoken languages that for two languages to be considered dialects of each other, at least 81% of their lexicon must be identical (Gudschinsky 1964). Our study, however, does not add up the percentage of signs that are identical. Instead, it compares only one phonetic factor of signs—the direction of primary movement path—and the table above is based only on the chosen eleven unweighted characteristics, some of which reflect genetic clusterings (and ASL and LIS are genetically related), and some of which reflect diaspora/origin-bound clusterings (and ASL and LIS are both diaspora languages). Thus it could still well be

TABLE 6.1. Percentage of Relation Based on Characteristic Scoring

	ASL	BSL	LIS	LSF	Auslan
ASL		(2) 18%	(8) 73%	(6) 55%	(5) 45%
BSL			(1) 9%	(3) 27%	(8) 73%
LIS				(7) 64%	(4) 36%
LSF					(0) 0%
Auslan					

(and undoubtedly is) that BSL and Auslan are more alike overall than ASL and LIS, even though with respect to the eleven characteristics of the one phonetic factor of direction of primary movement included here, the couples in these pairs of languages may be equally similar to one another.

It could also be that the particular dictionaries we are using have slanted our data, as we discussed in chapter 2. Interestingly, though, this possibility is heartening to us in that it actually provides an argument for the validity of our approach. That is, despite differences in lexicographical methods used in these dictionaries, which have undoubtedly led to shortcomings in our corpora, the analytical approach we have offered here clarifies the profundity of the similarity between BSL and Auslan (even if to a slightly lesser extent than one might have hoped for).

The entire hierarchy above is, indeed, encouraging with respect to the promise of our approach for noting similarities between languages. Every pairing of genetically related languages is on one of the first three tiers. In fact, these tiers are reserved only for genetically related languages. This suggests the genetics first proposal.

Genetics First: Genetic relatedness is the most important factor in determining similarity among sign languages.

We notice LIS and ASL as a pair are higher on the hierarchy than are LSF and ASL as a pair. So sisters that are not only genetically related but also both diaspora languages are more similar than sisters that are merely genetically related. However, we also note that LSF and LIS as a pair are higher on the hierarchy than are LSF and ASL as a pair. Why should that be? Certainly, the sisters LSF and LIS are geographically closer to one another than the sisters LSF and ASL. We doubt, though, that the greater similarity of the first pair is due to frequency of contact. In fact, we hesitate to speculate about this at all.

On the fourth and fifth tiers in the Similarity Hierarchy we see pairs related by the fact that both are diaspora languages

(ASL and Auslan; LIS and Auslan), although they are not geneti-cally related. This suggests that being a diaspora language is a strong factor in determining similarity.

> **Diaspora Second:** Being a diaspora language is the second most important factor in determining similarity among sign languages.

This is a radical new finding. The very idea that diaspora languages, even when genetically related, might cluster already flies in the face of tradi-tional historical linguistics. And now, the finding that being a diaspora language without genetic relatedness is such a strong characteristic in typologizing languages phonetically must be even more disturbing. We remind the reader that, as we argued in the section "Character-istics Distinguishing Origin-Bound from Diaspora Languages" of this chapter, with regard to primary path movement, the innovations found across the diaspora languages amount to exploiting freedom of path direction in the most readily available ways—which seems to us the most natural type of phonetic innovation. So these diaspora languages are clustering because of their innovative characteristics.

Notice that although ASL, Auslan, and LIS are all diaspora languages, ASL and Auslan share a common contact spoken lan-guage (English), which LIS does not share. This fact correlates with the fact that the ASL and Auslan pair is on a higher tier than the LIS and Auslan pair.

On the sixth tier we find the two origin-bound languages, BSL and LSF, together. Before doing this study, we might have expected these two languages to be on the very bottom tier. However, these languages fall together in being the languages with the lon-gest history in our study. We speculated earlier that they might be exhibiting characteristics held over from a very early stage in their development. That speculation, in fact, led us to propose that not only origin-bound languages favor **Away** (a generaliza-tion that emerges from our data), but young languages do as well (a hypothesis we put to the test in chapter 7).

On the seventh tier we find BSL and ASL. These are genetically unrelated languages—one is an origin-bound language and the other is a diaspora language—but they share a contact spoken language.

The pairs of languages on the bottom two tiers that have the least in common (LIS and BSL; LSF and Auslan) are in different genetic families, clash with respect to the origin-bound/diaspora split, and do not share a contact spoken language.

7

TESTING AND BEYOND

In this chapter we test the proposals we arrived at in chapter 6 on a sixth language, Nicaraguan Sign Language/*idioma de señas de Nicaragua* (ISN), taking up those proposals in the order in which they appear in chapter 6.

First, we will test for our claimed universals, involving adaptive modularity and anchors, as well as for any uniformity we saw across all the languages (such as with the curve signs). We could have used any sign language to test in these regards.

We chose ISN in particular to measure the validity of the analytic approach employed in arriving at other proposals of ours with respect to three specific factors. First, the contact spoken language is Spanish, a Romance language that has been claimed to be a high-frequency-gesture language; so looking at ISN is relevant to those characteristics we found that were sensitive to contact languages. Second, ISN has had considerable contact with ASL, since American scholars have been involved in the school in Managua, Nicaragua, continuously since the mid-1980s. Whether this contact is strong enough for ISN to be genetically related to ASL is unknown, however. We therefore will look at how it behaves with respect to our analytical tools in the hopes that others can confirm or disconfirm our finding (that is, our determination of genetic relatedness or not) in independent ways. Third, ISN is a very young language, so our (highly speculative) proposal about young languages (Young Favors **Away**) can be tested.

We end the chapter (and the book) with suggestions for future research.

Generalizations across Languages

Anchors/Goals and Adaptive Modularity

Our study of the other five languages led us to the anchor principle, repeated here.

> **Anchor Principle:** Signs favor movement toward an anchor or goal. For 1H signs, the goal is the signer. For 2HIB signs, the goal is the base hand. For 2H signs that involve reflexive symmetry across a plane (regardless of which plane), the goal (which is bipolar) is the plane of symmetry.

So let's see if goals appear in ISN.

In figure 7.1 through 7.3 we see the ISN Venn diagrams for the three major types of signs: 1H, 2HIB, and 2HRM. Looking at these figures, we find that 1H signs do favor **Ts** when compared with any other cardinal direction (that is, uncombined direction). For 2HIB

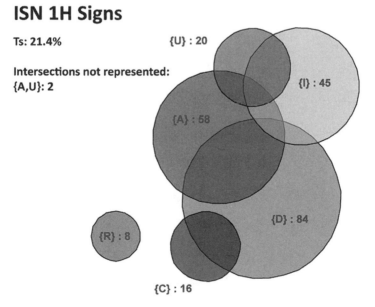

ISN 1H Signs

Ts: 21.4%

{U} : 20

Intersections not represented:
{A,U}: 2

{I} : 45

{A} : 58

{D} : 84

{R} : 8

{C} : 16

Figure 7.1. ISN 1H Noncurve Signs

(A = **Away**; U = **Up**; I = **Ipsil**; D = **Down**; R = **Rear**; C = **Contral**)

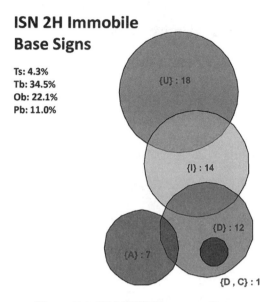

Figure 7.2. ISN 2HIB Noncurve Signs
(A = **Away**; U = **Up**; I = **Ipsil**; D = **Down**; R = **Rear**; C = **Contral**;
OnB = On the base; **PastB** = Past the base)

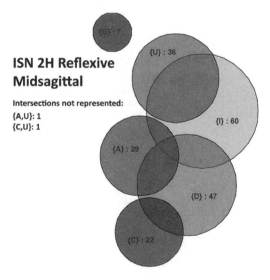

Figure 7.3. ISN 2HRM Noncurve Signs
(A = **Away**; U = **Up**; I = **Ipsil**; D = **Down**; R = **Rear**;
C = **Contral**; B = **Back**)

signs, the base hand (that is, the combined direction of **Tb-OnB-PastB**) is overwhelmingly favored. For 2HRM signs, again, the plane of symmetry is, indeed, favored. So the existence of goals is confirmed. We suspect that these findings are the unmarked case for sign languages, and we are gratified in that finding, since our account of goals in chapter 6 was based on considerations of motor coordination. There is more to be said here, however, and we will return to the issue of goals after looking at the issue of adaptive modularity.

In terms of the overall geography of the intersections, ISN looks very much like ASL for 1H signs. However, for 2HIB signs ISN shows differences from the other languages in our study, most notably because **Away** does not combine widely (but rather only with **Down**), and, second, because **Contral** occurs only in combination with **Down**. And for 2HRM signs, ISN shows differences from the other languages, most notably because many fewer combinations of directions occur in general, and, again, because **Away** does not combine as widely as it does in the other languages.

In 1H signs, **Away, Down,** and **Ipsil** all combine with three other directions. In 2HIB signs, **Down** combines with two other directions and subsumes a third, whereas **Ipsil** combines with two other directions. In 2HRM signs, **Ipsil** and **Down** combine with three other directions, but **Away** combines with only two and **Up** and **Contral** combine with only one. ISN, then, does not conform perfectly to the adaptive modularity hierarchy we arrived at by looking at the other five languages. In particular, with respect to ISN, we find the following:

Adaptive Modularity Hierarchy for ISN

For 1H:	GOAL > **Away** > **Down** > **Ipsil** > **Up** > **Contral** > **Rear**
For 2HIB:	GOAL > **Down** > **Ipsil** > {**Up, Away, Contral**}
For 2HRM:	{**Down, Ipsil**} > **Away** > {**Up, Contral**} > **Back**
Overall hierarchy:	GOAL > **Down** > **Ipsil** > **Away** > **Up** > **Contral** > {**Rear, Back**}

The overall hierarchy for ISN differs from the overall hierarchy we arrived at in chapter 6 for the other five languages primarily by one fact: **Away** has less adaptive modularity in ISN than it does in the other languages—it has moved down the hierarchy from a position immediately after the goal. And this happens because, although **Away** has the highest (except for the goal) adaptive modularity for 1H signs, it does not have the highest adaptive modularity for either 2HIB or 2HRM signs, with **Down** and even **Ipsil** being more adaptive. The relative consistency of the rest of the hierarchy, however, is heartening. It looks like **Away** and **Down**, although they may vary in which is more adaptive than the others, will consistently be of higher (or equal) adaptive modularity as **Up** and **Contral** across sign languages; **Rear** and **Back** show little to no ability to combine with other directions, and **Ipsil** is the wild card here (sometimes showing high adaptive modularity, sometimes showing low adaptive modularity).

We therefore revise our general hierarchy here, keeping precision for 1H signs, but building in variation for the other two types of signs:

Revised Adaptive Modularity Hierarchy

For 1H:	GOAL > **Away** > **Down** > **Ipsil** > **Up** > **Contral** > **Rear**
For 2HIB:	GOAL > {**Away, Down**} > [**Ipsil**] > {**Up, Contral**}
For 2HRM:	{**Away, Down**} > [**Ipsil**] > {**Up, Contral**} > **Back**
Overall hierarchy:	GOAL > {**Away, Down**} > [**Ipsil**] > {**Up, Contral**} > {**Rear, Back**}

This is to be understood as indicating that for 1H signs, there is a distinct cline in adaptive modularity across the directions, whereas for 2HIB and 2HRM signs the directions **Away** and **Down** will be relatively higher than **Up** and **Contral**, which will be relatively higher than **Rear** and **Back**. Directions within curly brackets, however, need not be of equal adaptiveness; depending on the language, they might be equal or either might be more adaptive than the other. Furthermore, the direction **Ipsil**, marked with square brackets, can move up or down the hierarchy to the adjacent level of adaptiveness, depending on the language. And that variability is reflected in our statement of the overall hierarchy.

The difference in the relative positions of **Away** and **Down** between our original adaptive modularity hierarchy and the hierarchy for ISN alone prompted us to take a second look at the issue of goals. For 2HIB signs, if we compare **Tb-OnB-PastB** with combinations of directions (rather than purely cardinal directions), for all six languages it is clear that **Tb-OnB-PastB** is the massively heavy anchor—the unchallenged goal. For 2HRM signs, if we compare the sum of combinations of **Ipsil** and **Contral** to the sum of combinations for any of the other directions, again **Ipsil** and **Contral** handily win for all six languages. So the plane of symmetry is the goal. However, when we turn to 1H signs, if we compare **Ts** to combinations of the other directions rather than simply to cardinal directions, we find that in ASL, **Away** wins by a slight margin (103 to 95); in BSL **Away** wins strongly (266 to 102); in LIS **Ts** wins by a slight margin (86 to 82); in LSF **Away** wins by a slight margin (139 to 115); in Auslan **Away** wins by a slight margin (158 to 142); in ISN **Down** wins strongly (84 to 48). In other words, with this combination approach, the goal is (with the exception of LIS) the direction with the greatest adaptive modularity: **Away** for ASL, BSL, LSF, and Auslan, and **Down** for ISN.

We conclude that 1H signs differ from the other two major types of signs with respect to goals. We are led to this hypothesis:

> **Goal in 1H:** In 1H signs, **Ts** and the direction of greatest adaptive modularity will vie for being the goal.

Curves

With respect to curve paths, we found for the other five languages that when symmetry was defined across a plane other than the Mid (the unmarked plane), only curves visible in the plane of symmetry are found. We called this "the curve markedness constraint." It turns out that there are no curve signs in our ISN database that exhibit symmetry across any plane other than the Mid plane (see appendix D and tables D.3 and D.4). So the curve markedness constraint can be considered to be trivially confirmed in ISN.

Turning now to issues of prevalence of CW versus CCW, we noted for the other five languages that for 1H curve signs, if curves are visible on the Mid plane, CW is favored; if curves are visible on the HZ plane, CCW is favored; if curves are visible on the VW plane, CW is preferred by all but LSF.

Further we found that with respect to all three types of signs, when the curve is visible on the Mid plane, CW is favored—strongly with 1H signs and variably with the other two major types of signs.

When it comes to curves visible on the HZ plane, four of the languages favor CCW movement across the three types of signs, with the exception that BSL shows no favor on 1H signs and LSF shows no favor on 2HIB signs. Auslan stands apart from the other languages, however, in favoring CCW for 1H and 2HRM signs, but CW for 2HIB signs.

Likewise, when it comes to curves visible on the VW plane, the data do not lend themselves to generalizations.

So now let's see where ISN falls in all this. The raw data on curve signs in ISN are given in appendix C (tables C.6, C.12, and C.18) and are summed up in table 7.1.

Just as with the other five languages, when 1H curves are visible on the Mid plane, CW is favored. However, when they are visible on the HZ plane, we find no favoritism; still, we note that this is a small data sampling. And when they are visible on the VW plane, CW is (heavily) favored. Overall, then, 1H curves behave (largely) as expected.

Second, just as with the other five languages, when the curve is visible on the Mid plane, CW is favored across all three types of signs (and very strongly for 1H signs).

TABLE 7.1. ISN Curve Signs

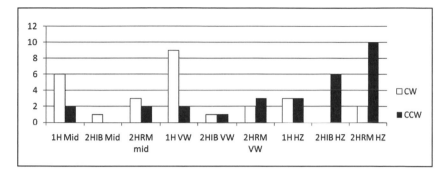

Third, just as with the other five languages (with some exceptions), when the curve is visible on the HZ plane, CCW is favored for 2HIB and 2HRM signs (strongly for both). However, there is no favoritism for 1H signs (and, as we said, the sampling is small).

Fourth, just as with the other five languages, the full range of variability is found when the curve is visible on the VW plane.

That ISN should be so consistent with the other five languages when it comes to curve signs reinforces our idea that curve data may be more influenced by physiological and visual factors than by phonetic factors.

Characteristics by Which ISN Stands Apart from the Others

First, immediately apparent is the fact that ISN allows less combining of directions than the other languages. We note that ASL allowed the least combining of direction for 2HIB signs. These facts make us wonder whether young sign languages might do less combining of directions than more seasoned sign languages. BSL and LSF are the oldest languages in our study. Next is LIS, which could be considered to date from 1784, when Tommaso Silvestri returned from studying people who were deaf in Paris and opened the doors of the first Deaf school in Rome (initially in the house of the lawyer Pasquale Di Pietro and eventually transferred to the present site in Via Nomentana). After that comes ASL, with the founding of the first Deaf school in Hartford in 1817; and then Auslan, with the founding of the first Deaf school in Sydney in 1860 (Thomas Pattison's school). ISN is by far the youngest of the languages in our study, dating back only to 1977. The fact that Auslan is younger than ASL (if we reckon solely by the date of the establishment of these schools), however, would go against our speculation, since Auslan has the most combining of directions for 2HIB signs (whereas ASL has the least).

To find further characteristics by which ISN stands apart from the other languages, we integrated it into the various tables presented in earlier chapters and in the appendices. Here is what we found out.

First, we noted earlier that Auslan stands apart from the other five languages in having heavy use of 1H swings. When we compare ISN, we find it has even heavier use of 1H swings (percentage-wise), plus it has heavy use of 2HIB swings, and the only language that outstrips it for 2HRM swings is Auslan. We conclude that a unique characteristic of ISN is heavy use of swings across all three sign types (unlike Auslan, which shows no 2HIB swings in our database), and this can be seen in table 7.2, where swing signs are shown as a percentage of all noncurve signs of each of the three relevant sign types (this table is an augmented version of table 3.2 from chapter 3). Among 2HIB noncurve signs that are not swings, ISN stands out from all five other languages in its

TABLE 7.2. **Swing Signs as Percentages of Noncurve Signs**

	1H Swings	2HIB Swings	2HRM Swings
ASL	0.3%	0.8%	10.6%
BSL	0.7%	0.3%	11.6%
LIS	0.7%	0.6%	14.4%
LSF	2.6%	0.0%	13.0%
Auslan	4.8%	0.0%	17.6%
ISN	5.9%	2.2%	19.4%

distribution of signs across **Tb, OnB,** and **PastB**, with much less use of **Tb**. Further, ISN makes considerable use of **PastB** as compared with **OnB** (making it more like LIS and LSF). To see this, we integrate data from ISN into table 3.1 of chapter 3, yielding table 7.3. (Recall that to get the comparison of **Tb** cf. **OnB**, for example, divide the difference between the number of **Tb** and **OnB** signs by the number of **OnB** signs. Note that **Tb** is greater than **OnB** in the given proportion.)

With respect to 1H, 2HIB, and 2HRM curve signs, ISN distributes them differently from the other five languages: nearly half of all ISN curve signs are 1H signs, and relatively few (only 17%) are 2HIB signs. We can see this by integrating ISN into table C.22 from appendix C and then converting the numbers of signs (shown in parentheses) into percentages, as shown in table 7.4.

Further, ISN generally makes less use of curve signs than the other languages do, as seen in table 7.5 (an augmented version of table 4.2). When we run a chi-square test on the data behind table 7.5, we find an extremely highly significant difference ($\chi^2 = 81.9$; ***$p < .0001$). Clearly, ASL, BSL, and Auslan cluster here, whereas

TABLE 7.3. 2HIB Noncurve Signs Excluding Swings

	Tb	OnB	PastB	Sum (Tb, OnB, PastB)	Tb cf. OnB	OnB cf. PastB
ASL	43%	28%	5%	76%	0.54	4.25
BSL	51%	23%	7%	81%	1.18	2.35
LIS	50%	13%	8%	70%	3.00	0.57
LSF	41%	19%	12%	72%	1.17	0.53
Auslan	39%	36%	5%	79%	0.06	5.73
ISN	34%	25%	13%	72%	0.36	0.96

(Please recall that the discrepancy between column three and the sums of the first three columns for LIS and Auslan is a result of rounding to the nearest percentile for the first three columns.)

TABLE 7.4. Distribution of Curve Signs

	ASL	BSL	LIS	LSF	Auslan	ISN	Total
1H	(49)	(51)	(85)	(84)	(81)	(26)	376
	36%	30%	43%	41%	39%	49%	
2HIB	(36)	(46)	(38)	(56)	(65)	(9)	250
	26%	27%	22%	27%	31%	17%	
2HRM	(53)	(73)	(74)	(64)	(63)	(18)	345
	38%	43%	38%	31%	30%	34%	
Total	138	170	197	204	209	53	971

LIS, LSF, and ISN do not. In fact, LIS makes the heaviest use of curves and ISN makes the lightest use. We note, very circumspectly, that the cluster is of the languages with English as their contact spoken language. We have no explanation for this; perhaps it is a random occurrence.

With respect to symmetries other than 2HRM, we find that ISN makes no use of the VW plane in our data set—for neither non-curve nor curve signs. And ISN makes use of the HZ plane only for noncurve signs. On both these points it is unique as compared with the other five languages. Further, it has only one rotation sign with primary movement (although there are others with just a wrist twist). However, overall, ISN makes similar low usage of these symmetries to the other languages (less than 2%), with the already noted exception that ASL revels in these symmetries. Chi-square statistical analysis shows that the six languages are

TABLE 7.5. Curve Sign Summary

	Curves
ASL	11%
BSL	11%
LIS	21%
LSF	15%
Auslan	12%
ISN	7%

extremely highly significantly different ($\chi^2 = 25.5$; ***$p < .0001$). We find that by removing the ASL data, which was an outlier before, chi-square statistical analysis shows a 47% chance that the remaining five languages are the same ($\chi^2 = 3.5$; $p = .47$). So ASL is still the outlier, and ISN is like the other languages in this regard.

Characteristics That Languages Cluster Around

We now turn to the eleven characteristics that we found most useful in comparing the other five languages to see how ISN behaves with respect to them.

Characteristics Distinguishing Genetic Families

Fully five of the eleven characteristics discussed in chapter 6 distinguish members of one genetic family from the other genetic family, and those characteristics cut across all three major types of signs. If ISN belongs to the LSF family (that is, if the influence of ASL is that strong, a question that arises given the history of the school where the dictionary we used was made), we predict that ISN will fall with the LSF family here. Let's go through these five characteristics one by one.

1. For 1H noncurve signs, the BSL family uses **Ipsil** much less frequently than the LSF family. ISN falls with the LSF family here, as the similarity of figure 7.1 to figure 3.1 shows. Statistics support this conclusion: the six languages differ significantly ($\chi^2 = 16.6$; *$p < .05$). Additional testing revealed ASL, LIS, LSF, and ISN to have an 85% chance of being the same ($\chi^2 = 0.81$; $p = .85$), whereas BSL and Auslan now show a 60% chance of being the same ($\chi^2 = 0.27$; $p = .60$).

2. The geography of 2HIB noncurve signs with respect to adaptive modularity splits on genetic lines quite neatly. ISN does not fall with either family, showing much less adaptive modularity overall, and showing both **Ipsil** and **Down** to have greater adaptive modularity than **Away**.

3. For 2HIB noncurve base signs (combining **Tb, PastB**, and **OnB**), the BSL family has a significantly higher prevalence than the LSF family. ISN falls with the LSF family on this point, as we saw in table 7.3.

4. With 2HRM noncurve signs, the LSF family uses **Contral** much more than the BSL family. ISN goes with the BSL family on this, as a comparison of figure 7.3 with figures 3.14 through 3.18 shows. Statistics supports this conclusion: for **Contral** there is a highly significant contrast in the six languages ($\chi^2 = 17.8$; **p <.005). LSF, LIS, and ASL now exhibit a 67% chance of being the same ($\chi^2 = 0.79$; $p = .67$), whereas BSL, Auslan, and ISN exhibit a 7% chance of being the same ($\chi^2 = 5.3$; $p = .07$).

5. In two-handed symmetrical signs (including all types of symmetries), the BSL family makes significantly more use of connected hands than the LSF family. ISN, on the other hand, has only four 2HRM noncurve signs with connected hands and only one translation sign with connected hands, adding up to less than 1% of the overall signs (.006). In fact, ISN falls with the LSF family here, although not robustly. There is a highly significant difference among the six languages ($\chi^2 = 22.0$; **p <.005). When we perform additional chi-square tests, we find ASL, LIS, LSF, and ISN have a 19% chance of being the same ($\chi^2 = 4.8$; $p = .19$), whereas BSL and Auslan now have a 90% chance of being the same ($\chi^2 = 0.02$; $p = .90$).

In sum, ISN falls with the LSF family strongly on two of these characteristics and unremarkably on one, with the BSL family very slightly on one, and with neither on one. Although this is not random behavior, it is also not convincing evidence for a genetic relationship. This might be the behavior we would expect if ISN borrowed heavily from the LSF family (which we know it did, via ASL) but was not genetically related. This finding is important. It suggests that these five characteristics really do help to distinguish the BSL family from the LSF family and are not accidental results or artifacts of any idiosyncrasies in our database or methodology of analysis.

Characteristics Distinguishing Origin-Bound from Diaspora Languages

Three of the eleven characteristics discussed in chapter 6 distinguish origin-bound languages from diaspora languages, and all of them concern 1H signs. Let us summarize them here.

1. Origin-bound languages use **Away** much more prevalently in 1H noncurve signs than diaspora languages do.
2. Origin-bound languages use **Down** more prevalently in 1H noncurve signs than the others do.
3. In terms of the overall geography of the intersections of path directions for 1H noncurve signs, origin-bound languages form one cluster and diaspora languages form another, differences being in the relative size of the various intersections.

On the basis of the first characteristic, we came up with the following proposal.

> **Young Favors Away:** Young sign languages will make heavy use of **Away** in 1H signs.

It is difficult even to ask whether ISN is an origin-bound or diaspora language, since its genetic relatedness to the LSF family is not firmly determined. If it were clearly genetically related to ASL, it would be a diaspora language and should pattern accordingly.

In any case, ISN is a young language, in fact, an extremely young language. Therefore, we predict that in 1H signs ISN will make heavy use of **Away**, as young languages should by the proposal Young Favors **Away**. And we make no predictions about its use of **Down** or how the geography of the intersections of path directions will compare with that of the other languages in this study.

In fact, ISN does make heavy use of **Away**, confirming our proposal. However, it makes even heavier use of **Down**. We recall that in chapter 6 we considered making the proposal Young Favors **Down**, but we hesitated because, although the differences in the groups were statistically significant, the coherence of each group regarding the prevalence of **Down** was not as overwhelming as it was with respect to the prevalence of **Away**. We now backtrack and add in that proposal.

> **Young Favors Down:** Young sign languages will make heavy use of **Down** in 1H signs.

With respect to the third characteristic, 1H signs in ISN show a very similar geography to 1H signs in ASL, as we have already noted repeatedly. Here ISN goes with the diaspora languages. Given our approach, this is a random fact; it could as easily have gone with neither group or with the origin-bound languages.

Characteristics Distinguished by Contact Spoken Language

Two of the eleven characteristics discussed in chapter 6 distinguish languages whose contact spoken language is English from languages whose contact spoken language is French or Italian. Let us repeat them here.

1. With 2HIB noncurve signs, LIS and LSF make significantly more use of **Ipsil** than the other three languages.
2. BSL and Auslan are almost identical to one another in the geography of 2HIB noncurve signs and in the extent to which they make use of these signs. ASL makes even higher use of these signs. LSF and, especially, LIS make lower use of these signs.

We suggested that these two characteristics followed from the fact that English is spoken in low-frequency-gesture cultures whereas French and Italian are spoken in high-frequency-gesture cultures. (An alternative explanation that others have offered us is that BSL and Auslan use a two-handed alphabet, whereas LSF and LIS use a one-handed alphabet. This account, however, leaves us at a loss for why ASL, which has a one-handed alphabet, patterns with BSL and Auslan on both of these characteristics.)

The dominant contact spoken language for ISN is Spanish, and it is spoken in a high-frequency-gesture culture (Pika, Nicoladis, and

Marentette 2006). We therefore predict that ISN will behave similarly to LIS and LSF here. (And notice that ISN uses a one-handed alphabet—so, unfortunately, it gives us no further information about whether the contact spoken language or the type of alphabet is the important factor.)

In fact, ISN does make high use of **Ipsil** in 2HIB noncurve signs. And when we run the statistics for **Ipsil**, we find there is an extremely highly significant difference among the six languages ($\chi^2 = 38.7$; ***$p < .0001$). However, we see no statistically significant clustering among any of the languages. So, although ISN is like LIS and LSF in making high use of **Ipsil**, and although it contrasts with ASL, BSL, and Auslan on this feature, this is not a statistically significant result.

Finally, when we compare ISN to the other languages with respect to the percentage of signs that are noncurve 2HIB out of all the signs with primary movement in our study, we find that ISN, against expectations, clusters with BSL and Auslan, excluding ASL, as shown in table 7.6 (which is an augmented form of table 3.4 from chapter 3). In fact, the six languages are extremely highly significantly different ($\chi^2 = 48.7$; ***$p < .0001$). BSL, Auslan, and ISN, however, are strongly similar to one another on prevalence of 2HIB signs ($\chi^2 = 0.46$; $p = .80$), but the remaining languages still show an extremely highly significant difference ($\chi^2 = 45.3$; ***$p < .0001$).

Our predictions do not hold, thus calling into question our suggestions about the effect of contact spoken language on the phonetics of 2HIB signs. Further, these results are just as incon-

TABLE 7.6. Noncurve Signs as Percentage of All Signs

	1H Signs	2HIB Signs	2HRM Signs
ASL	29%	30%	25%
BSL	30%	25%	28%
LIS	31%	18%	27%
LSF	30%	21%	30%
Auslan	30%	26%	28%
ISN	33%	26%	29%

sistent with any account of these phonetic data that points to one-handed versus two-handed alphabet languages.

Characteristics Revealing Other Clusterings

The final characteristic discussed in chapter 6 groups Auslan, BSL, and LIS together, in contrast to ASL and LSF. We summarize it here:

> For 2HIB noncurve signs, with respect to **Down**, ASL and LSF pattern together, using it more prevalently, whereas LIS, BSL, and Auslan pattern together (with LIS using **Down** the least).

Since this finding was arbitrary as far as we could see, we make no predictions about where ISN would fall. When we threw the data from all six languages together, our initial test showed no statistical difference ($\chi^2 = 11.0$; $p = .051$). Since the p-value is so close to statistically significant, we ran a different test (the likelihood ratio test), which did show a statistically significant difference ($\chi^2 = 11.6$; $p < .05$). At that point, we ran ASL, LSF, and ISN together, and they showed a statistically significant clustering, as against LIS, BSL, and Auslan. However, when we ran ASL and LSF as against LIS, BSL, Auslan, and ISN, we also found two clusters. That is, ISN could go either way. In other words, what we really found was not clusters, but clutter. This particular characteristic, then, cannot be included in our final comparison in the rest of this chapter. We greet this conclusion with relief, since the original finding led us to make a grouping for only a single characteristic—a grouping that, as far as we could see, did not correlate with any other factors about the languages.

Overview of How the Languages Cluster on These Characteristics

Based on how the languages clustered on the original eleven characteristics, we came up with the similarity hierarchy, and with two proposals, repeated here.

> **Genetics First:** Genetic relatedness is the most important factor in determining similarity among sign languages.

> **Diaspora Second:** Being a diaspora language is the second most important factor in determining similarity among sign languages.

Given those findings, if ISN is not genetically related to ASL, then it is in neither the LSF nor the BSL family. Further, it is not a diaspora language. And, finally, the spoken language around it is a high-gesture language. So we are led to certain expectations of where it should appear on the similarity hierarchy. In fact, we would expect the pairing of ISN and LSF to be at a higher level than any other pairing with ISN, since they both have high-gesture contact spoken languages and young languages, like ISN, should pattern with origin-bound languages on certain characteristics (which is the hypothesis that led us to propose the principle Young Favors **Away** in the first place, and now the additional principle Young Favors **Down**). Consistently, we expect the pairing of ISN and Auslan to be the lowest pairing with ISN, since the two languages have no relevant factors in common.

On the other hand, if ISN is truly related to ASL, it is in the LSF family and it is a diaspora language. Ignoring anything but the factors we have deemed relevant thus far, we would predict the pairing of ISN and LIS to be the highest pairing that ISN is involved with (the languages being in the same family, being diaspora, and having a high-gesture contact spoken language), or the pairing of ISN and LSF to be the highest pairing that ISN is involved with (the languages being in the same family and having a high-gesture contact spoken language, but also having whatever it is that young languages and origin-bound languages share). However, given that ISN would, in this scenario, be a daughter of ASL, we might instead expect that the highest pairing would be ISN with ASL, and the pairings ISN with LIS and ISN with LSF would not be far behind. Consistently, we would expect the pairing of ISN with BSL (having in common whatever it is that young languages and origin-bound languages share) and the pairing of ISN with Auslan (both being diaspora languages) to be at equal (or close) levels and to be the lowest pairings.

In table 7.7 we compare all six languages now on ten characteristics (skipping the eleventh, which was cast into doubt) in the same way we did for the original five languages in table 6.1 of chapter 6. If we now insert the ISN data, we find a new similarity hierarchy:

Similarity Hierarchy for All Six Languages

LIS and LSF/LIS and ASL

BSL and Auslan

LSF and ASL/ISN and LSF

Auslan and ASL/ISN and ASL/ISN and BSL/ISN and LIS

BSL and LSF/LIS and Auslan/ISN and Auslan

BSL and ASL

LIS and BSL/LSF and Auslan

There are now only seven levels, compared with nine in the original hierarchy; so the effect of dropping the eleventh characteristic is evidenced in finding more inhabitants on a given level. Levels 1 and 2 of the old hierarchy have been conflated (with a difference that we will return to); levels 5 and 6 have been conflated; and levels 8 and 9 have been conflated. The important difference, however, is that BSL and Auslan are now lower in the similarity hierarchy than both LIS and ASL, and LIS and LSF. This is a disturbing result, given that BSL and Auslan are mutually comprehensible whereas the other pairs are not.

Strikingly, the pairings with ISN are as expected if ISN is not genetically related to ASL. So if our methodological approach in this

TABLE 7.7. Percentage of Relation Based on Characteristic Scoring

	ASL	BSL	LIS	LSF	Auslan	ISN
ASL		(1) 10%	(8) 80%	(5) 50%	(4) 40%	(4) 40%
BSL			(0) 0%	(3) 30%	(7) 70%	(4) 40%
LIS				(8) 80%	(3) 30%	(4) 40%
LSF					(0) 0%	(5) 50%
Auslan						(3) 30%
ISN						

book is on the right track, then other methods for evaluating genetic relatedness should also judge ISN to not be in the LSF family.

Conclusions

The study of ISN presented some differences with respect to the adaptive modularity hierarchy and led us to a revision of the hierarchy as well as to a better understanding of goals in 1H signs.

It also allowed us to conflate several levels of the similarity hierarchy. We find this a positive result. Nine levels (in the original hierarchy) for comparing only five languages seemed to claim a refinement of comparison that was too strong for the very gross nature of this study (which looks only at direction of movement). Seven levels (in the new hierarchy) for comparing six languages are moving us in the right direction.

One might be surprised that, with our approach, the evidence for a genetic relationship between ISN and ASL is lacking. If our results can be borne out by other methods of judging genetic relatedness, this suggests that the role of home signs in ISN was strong enough to give it a foundation.

We are particularly excited by the fact that the very young language of ISN does use **Away** and **Down** more heavily than diaspora languages tend to do. Findings of that sort suggest that there are fundamentals of sign phonetics (here, the directions **Away** and **Down**) that new languages use heavily and that over time other factors (here, other directions) enter or become more active; so the phonetics of mature diaspora languages (and perhaps of mature but innovative origin-bound languages) can be expected to be more complex in certain senses than the phonetics of both young languages and mature but conservative origin-bound languages.

Suggestions for Future Research

Our particular research trio has scattered, so we cannot pursue further study in this area together. We suggest work that we hope others will carry out (some of which one or a pair of us might pursue).

It would be useful to carry out a study in which conversations in the six sign languages studied here were videotaped and then the handshapes were masked (perhaps with all movement being reduced to points of light, as in Poizner, Bellugi, and Lutes-Driscoll 1981), so that viewers could see only the parameters of location and movement. This would direct the viewers' attention to the path of movement. One could then have signers from the various languages watch the videos and make judgments about sameness. Our work would predict that viewers should be able to identify their own language and might very well judge genetically related languages to be "the same" as their own. However, the farther down two languages are on the similarity hierarchy, the less likely it should be that viewers who are signers of one of the languages would judge the other language to be "the same."

Other studies also beg to be carried out. In that regard, some of our data lumps might be teased apart to fruitful ends. For example, across the languages many 1H signs fall in the **Ts** set; point of origin of movement could prove interesting. The same can be said for the set labeled **Tb** for 2HIB noncurve signs. And for the set labeled **PastB**, both the origin and endpoint of movement might be worth investigating.

Length of movement path has not been considered in this study. Our BSL dictionary had a symbol indicating a quick tap. None of the other dictionaries used this symbol. We assumed the tap was a primary movement with a straight path, just a short one, perhaps no different from the path in the ASL sign MOTHER, for example. In fact, all the 1H signs we marked as repeated straight paths on the tables in our appendices are taps. In this work we do not take into account path length, but that could be a fertile topic for future work. It might turn out that taps are one way of recognizing BSL, since it has a high preponderance of taps. Our impression, however, is that

ASL and LIS also have many taps (even though the dictionaries did not indicate this).

The interaction of secondary movements and paths begs to be studied with respect to the findings here. We note that secondary movement or handshape change can occur once during a primary movement or multiple times during that movement, to noticeably different effect. LSF, for example, has signs in which alternating wrist rotations with an A- or S-handshape are repeated throughout the primary movement, adding a distinctive beat. Auslan has several signs in which alternating wrist rotations with a 5-handshape are repeated throughout the primary movement, giving a visual sense of rocking.

Likewise, we looked neither at hand orientation nor at handshape, but the interaction of each (particularly hand orientation) with direction of primary movement could yield interesting results since certain physiological combinations might be more or less comfortable. We might expect, then, that a given orientation and/or handshape would be more common with certain movement paths.

Finally, and most important of all, the analytical methods we employed show promise and merit being put to the test on additional languages. Languages related to either of the families already in the study would give us information on how strongly our results really do characterize these families, and languages unrelated to either of these families and, further, genetically related to one another, would give us information on how well our methodology helps to typologize languages. Young languages are of interest, since we make pointed predictions about them. Languages with a two-handed manual alphabet whose contact spoken language is a high-frequency-gesture language (if any exist) and languages with a one-handed alphabet whose contact spoken language is a low-frequency-gesture language (if any exist) would be valuable to test.

Village sign languages, both mature ones (in communities that have been using them for centuries, such as Al-Sayyid Bedouin Sign

Language of Israel, which has been around since the 1800s) and relatively young ones (such as Ban Khor Sign Language of Thailand, which has been around approximately eighty years) are largely unaffected by contact with outside sign languages, so they would offer ideal examples of languages unrelated to the families already in our study. Considering Adamorobe Sign Language and Ghanaian Sign Language, for example, would allow a genetic comparison, and Victoria Nyst tells us she is undertaking a long-term dictionary project right now.

In appendix E, we list resources we hope will be of help to the reader (and we thank an anonymous reviewer for this list).

We have an important caveat for future researchers: although the studies we suggest are of phonetics, one needs to know the meaning of the signs to be analyzed. Some dictionaries, such as *The Thai Sign Language Dictionary* (Suwanarat et al. 1990), must be sifted carefully. This dictionary lists as separate entries signs that are predictably related. For example, it has entries such as A VEHICLE, CARS PARKED SIDE BY SIDE, A VEHICLE MOVING AHEAD ON A HILLY ROAD, A VEHICLE MOVING AHEAD ON A ROUGH BUMPY ROAD, A VEHICLE SLOWLY CLIMBING AN INCLINE, A VEHICLE SLOWLY ENTERING A SHELTER, A VEHICLE TURNING RIGHT, A VEHICLE OVERTAKING ANOTHER, TWO VEHICLES RACING, A TRAFFIC JAM, and on and on, including various types of street accidents with people being thrown various directions (pages 100–108). And this is typical of the dictionary in general. In other words, the dictionary authors build the syntax of the language into the individual entries, making it as much (or more) an introduction to Thai Sign Language as it is a dictionary proper. It is therefore essential when approaching a dictionary of a sign language unfamiliar to the researchers to have translations of all the signs, so that the frozen lexicon (the object of study) can be distinguished from the productive lexicon.

Appendix A
Raw Data Not Included in the Figures in the Main Text

All the signs discussed in this appendix are included in the tables elsewhere that give totals of types of signs, with one exception: signs we list under the section "No Primary Movement" are not included in these tables.

No Primary Movement

Here we consider signs that have only secondary movement, only handshape change, only a combination of secondary movement and handshape change, or no movement whatsoever. The numbers of such 1H, 2HIB, and 2HRM signs are given in table A.1. Note that some of these signs are actually bisyllabic, but both of the syllables involve only secondary movement. Additionally, there are a handful of signs that do not fit into these three basic categories that have no primary movement, some of which are quite complex. For example, the sign DIE in ASL uses only secondary movement (wrist rotation),

TABLE A.1. Total Number of 1H, 2HIB, and 2HRM Signs Lacking Primary Movement

	1H	2HIB	2HRM	Totals
ASL	181	39	67	287
BSL	154	46	70	270
LIS	79	29	37	145
LSF	106	44	78	228
Auslan	214	53	106	373
Subtotals	734	211	358	1,303
ISN	88	45	89	220
Totals	822	256	447	1,525

but the hands are glided and symmetrical across the HZ plane, so if the movement were primary instead of secondary we would have a combination of two symmetries: rotation plus glide reflection.

Particularly Notable Phonetics (Motivated by Meaning)

We found four signs in this group, all 2HIB.

> **ASL:** AMONG: The G-handshape of the dominant hand wanders through the nondominant fingers.
> **BSL:** RIGHT-HANDED: The left hand taps the dominant forearm.
> SUBURBS: The dominant hand hops **Ipsil** a little ways, then hops **Contral** to the base hand.
> **ISN:** PIZZA: The dominant hand swings **PastB**, but on one part of the swing the path is simply straight and on the returning part it is Z.

Candidates for Polysyllabic Signs

Many signs with origins in compounds, mimicry, or drawing are open to a polysyllabic analysis. We discuss some of them here. Note that we do not include compounds in which each part is already in our database in this discussion.

In table A.2 we see the total numbers of potentially polysyllabic signs. Here we discuss them by type of sign for each language.

1H

> **BSL:** AUSTRALIA, BLUSH, CARE LESS, CATCH OFF GUARD, DISCOVER, GIANT, GRAFFITI, GREAT, ISLAND, SWITZERLAND.
> **LIS:** ANNULLARE ('annul').
> **LSF:** DEGOUTANT ('disgusting'), GRAND-MÈRE ('grandmother'), INVENTION ('invention'), ITALIQUE ('italic'), ÊTRE ('be') SALÉ ('salty'), SUISSE ('Switzerland').
> **Auslan:** ATTENTION, CATHOLIC, CHINA, FRANCE, FRUIT, FUSSY, SWITZERLAND.
> **ISN:** CAMELLO ('camel'), MISA ('mass'), SUIZA ('Switzerland').

TABLE A.2. Number of Potentially Polysyllabic Signs

	1H	2HIB	2H Both Move, Same Handshape	2HRM over Time	Totals
ASL		1	3		4
BSL	10	2	14		26
LIS	1				1
LSF	6	6			12
Auslan	7	2	7		16
Subtotals	24	11	24	0	59
ISN	3	3	3	2	11
Totals	27	14	27	2	70

2HIB

ASL: SCHEDULE.

BSL: CHRISTMAS, DIVERSION.

LSF: AUBERGINE ('eggplant'), BANANE ('banana'), FIL À PLOMB ('plumb line'), MACHINE À LAVER ('washing machine'), PARQUET ('parquet floor'), VIDEOPHONE ('videophone').

Auslan: CONFIDENTIAL, HOBART.

ISN: CALIENTE ('hot'), POLLITO ('chick'), VOTO/VOTAR ('vote').

2H Both Move, Same Handshape

ASL: One type of symmetry followed by a different type, or change in type of path shape, or change in plane of symmetry.

EXACT, KNOT, TEAR.

BSL: One hand exhibits secondary movement while both exhibit primary movement, or change in plane of symmetry, or change in path shape, or mix different types of symmetry, or hands do different path shapes.

ADORE, ALMIGHTY GOD, ATHLETICS, CHEF (which draws chef's hat, but could seem arbitrary to some), COMPETITION, DESTROY, DISORIENT, DIVERSE, HUNT, IMPOSSIBLE, INHERIT, LOVE, NURSE, SAIL.

Auslan: Hands change direction in a strange way or the type of symmetry changes.

DARWIN, GLASSES, GYM, JIGSAW, PINEAPPLE, SHIELD, VIETNAM.

ISN: 2HRM followed by 1H: CHOMPIPE (a type of turkey), CANGURO ('kangaroo'); also one 2HRM sign where the two hands come together (so the direction is **Contral**), then move in the direction **Away** in a ZZ path as a connected unit: LESBIANA ('lesbian'); also 1H (**Down** repeated) followed by 2HRM with a glide: BALONCESCO ('basketball').

2HRM over Time

ISN: One sign exhibits reflexivity over time, consisting of a first part that is 1H (**Ipsil** with an HH path shape) and a second part that is ChSi 2HIB: PERFUME ('PERFUME').

Appendix B
Raw Data Included in the Figures and Tables in the Main Text for Paths Other Than Curves for 1H, 2HIB, and 2HRM

Swing Signs

Information on swing signs for ASL, BSL, LIS, LSF, and Auslan is given in table B.1a.

There are several things to note regarding table B.1a:

Note 1. BSL: One 1H **Contral-Ipsil** swing goes **Contral**, then the hand rotates, then it swings back **Ipsil**.

Note 2. LIS: One 2HRM **Away-Back** swing included in this table is across the Mid plane rotated 45° to the left. One 2HRM **Contral-Ipsil** swing included in this table has the two hands come toward the plane then loop back away again, so the path shape is a very thinned-out loop.

Note 3. LSF: Two 2HRM **Away-Back** swings included in this table are across the Mid plane rotated 45° to the right. One 2HRM **Away-Down** swing included in this table is glided and the Mid plane is rotated 45° to the left; the hands move **Away-Down**, make a CW circle seen on the VW plane, then swing back. Two 2HRM **Contral-Ipsil** swings change height, so they swing toward the plane at one height, then swing back to a lower point from the one they started at: INCROYABLE ('incredible'), INSUPPORTABLE ('intolerable').

Note 4. Auslan: One 1H **Contral-Ipsil** swing included in this table has a secondary movement between phases of the swing (a mimic sign: SPRAY). One 2HRM **Away-Back** swing included in this table is a glide. Auslan also has some swings not included in this table (but they are included in the tables with totals in the main text): one elbow sign that swings Down-Up only once; two Mid glide reflections over time with swing movement, one Down-Up and the other AwayDown-BackUp.

Information on swing signs for all languages in this study (including ISN now) is given in table B.1b.

Note that for ISN several 2HRM swing signs are glided: one of the **Down-Up** signs; one of the **Contral-Ipsil** signs; one of the **Away-Back** signs; and one of the **AwayDown-BackUp** signs.

Ordinary Noncurve Path Signs

The data on these signs are given in tables B.2 through B.19. Sometimes movement is repeated. Within any column, figures in parentheses indicate the number of relevant signs with repeated movement.

Although in our analyses in the text we separated our signs into curve paths and noncurve paths only, when we first cataloged the signs we kept track of certain path characteristics. In the interests of others who might want to mine these data, we note these characteristics in the tables of this appendix. The symbols we used for the noncurve path characteristics are as follows:

ss = straight

H = a single hop or bounce from initial point to endpoint

HH = more than one hop or bounce from initial point to endpoint

~HH = inverted hops, so that you dip from one point to the next

jab = quick movement toward a point and back to the initial point (Dynamics sets jabs apart from a single swing.)

W = tiny undulations

WW = waves

WWW = one or more big exaggerated waves

Z = angle (sometimes curved at the apex)—apex can point Up, **Down**, or **Ipsil** (This subsumes what is often called "path shape 7.")

ZZ = zigzag (that is, multiple angles)

IF = initial flourish

FF = final flourish

G = glide

+45R or +45L = reflexive symmetry is across the Mid plane rotated 45° to the right or the left

The types of flourishes found differ by language:

ASL: Wrist rotation or circle (typically CW regardless of the plane the circle is seen on) before going straight.

LIS: Wrist rotation or circle (typically CCW regardless of the plane the circle is seen on) before going straight.

LSF: Curl before or after going straight (like on a candy cane) or initial arc then straight (which is different from the curl, because the straight line is not an unbroken continuation of the arc) or a (partial) loop before or after going straight.

Auslan: Curl before or after going straight (like on a candy cane).

Several notes must be made regarding these tables.

For table B.6: The repeated **Contral** wave is the sign FLYING SAUCER. No other language allows repeats on any path shape other than straight and the various curves, regardless of whether the signs are one-handed or two.

For table B.7 there are three notes:

Note 1. The final flourish indicated by * is a curve up at the end.

Note 2. The final flourish indicated by ** is a circle at the end, visible on the HZ plane, moving CCW.

Note 3. Many signs use a head movement as part of the sign.

One sign (ABEJA ['bee'], included in the chart) pushes the tongue against the cheek as the hand moves toward the cheek and makes a claw outside the cheek.

For table B.10: One of the **Tb** signs is really a swing **Tb** and back.

For table B.12 there are two notes:

Note 1. There is one sign not in the table that goes **Ipsil** then **Down** then **Ipsil** again.

Note 2. The **PastB** with an HH path hops onto the base then keeps going with hops in the air.

For table B.13: In one of the **PastB** signs (GRAMA ['creeping cynodon'— a type of grass]) only the nondominant hand has primary movement, while the dominant hand has only secondary movement.

For table B.19: Three of the **IpsilUp** signs cross the plane and one **Back** sign is cross the whole time.

TABLE B.1a. Total Number of Swing Signs per Direction for Five Languages

	ASL	BSL	LIS	LSF	Auslan	Totals
1H						
Away-Ts	0	0	0	3	3	6
Contral-Ipsil	0	3	2	3	20	28
Down-Contral	0	0	0	0	0	0
Down-Up	1	0	0	4	3	8
Ipsil-Up	0	0	0	0	0	0
AwayUp-Back-Down	0	0	0	1	0	1
ContralDown-IpsilUp	0	0	0	0	1	1
Subtotals	(1)	(3)	(2)	(11)	(27)	(44)
2HIB						
Down-Up	3	1	1	0	0	5
2HRM						
Away-Back	14	18	6	10	22	70
Contral-Ipsil	0	3	4	10	27	44
Down-Up	21	23	20	29	36	129
AwayDown-BackUp	0	3	0	4	3	10
AwayIpsil-BackContral	0	1	3	2	2	8
AwayUp-Back-Down	0	1	0	1	0	2
ContralDown-IpsilUp	0	2	2	1	3	8
ContralUp-IpsilDown	0	0	0	0	1	1
AwayDown-Ipsil-BackUp-Contral	0	0	4	2	0	6
Subtotals	(35)	(51)	(39)	(59)	(94)	(278)
Totals	39	55	42	70	121	327

TABLE B.1b. Total Number of Swing Signs per Direction for All Languages

	ASL	BSL	LIS	LSF	Auslan	Sub-totals	ISN	Total
1H								
Away-Ts	0	0	0	3	3	6	0	6
Contral-Ipsil	0	3	2	3	20	28	8	35
Down-Contral	0	0	0	0	0	0	1	1
Down-Up	1	0	0	4	3	8	4	12
Ipsil-Up	0	0	0	0	0	0	1	1
AwayUp-BackDown	0	0	0	1	0	1	0	1
Contral-Down-IpsilUp	0	0	0	0	1	1	0	1
Subtotals	(1)	(3)	(2)	(11)	(27)	(44)	(14)	(58)
2HIB								
Down-Up	3	1	1	0	0	5	4	9
2HRM								
Away-Back	14	18	6	10	22	70	8	78
Contral-Ipsil	0	3	4	10	27	44	5	49
Down-Up	21	23	20	29	36	129	25	154
Away-Down-BackUp	0	3	0	4	3	10	2	12
AwayIpsil-BackCon-tral	0	1	3	2	2	8	0	8
AwayUp-BackDown	0	1	0	1	0	2	0	2
Contral-Down-IpsilUp	0	2	2	1	3	8	0	8
Contral-Up-Ipsil-Down	0	0	0	0	1	1	0	1
Away-DownIp-sil-Back-UpContral	0	0	4	2	0	6	0	6
Subtotals	(35)	(51)	(39)	(59)	(94)	(278)	(40)	318
Totals	39	55	42	70	121	327	58	385

TABLE B.2. ASL 1H Signs

	Ts		Away				Contral		Down		Ipsil		Rear	Up
			-Down	-Ipsil	-Up	-Down Ipsil		-Down		-Ipsil		-Up		
S	47 (43)	39 (11)	19 (2)	11 (3)	4	1	8 (1)	2 (2)	27 (22)	4	20 (1)	7	6 (1)	10 (6)
H	1	5			1		7		10		16		1	3
HH	2	1											1	
Jab				1							1			
WWW			1											
Z		1	2						5		6			
ZZ			1						1					
IF	2													

TABLE B.3. BSL 1H Signs

	Ts		Away					Contral			Down			Ipsil		Rear	Up
			-Contral	-Down	-Ipsil	-Up	-Down Ipsil		-Down	-Up		-Ipsil	-Rear		-Up		
S	52 (50)	62 (17)	1	54 (5)	5	6 (1)	1	9 (2)	6 (3)	3	48 (20)	6	2	28	3		11 (6)
H								3	3		8			5		1	2
HH		1							1					2			
WW														4			
Z											3			3			
ZZ	2										1			2			

159

TABLE B.4. LIS 1H Signs

	Ts	Away							Contral		Down		Ipsil		Rear	Up
			−Down	−Ipsil	−Up	−Contral Down	−Down Ipsil	−Ipsil Up		−Down		−Ipsil		−Up		
S	27 (59)	35 (6)	17(3)	3	1	3	4	1	5 (8)	1	27 (21)	2	30 (6)	6 (1)	4	8 (2)
H		2						1	1						1	
W		1							1							
WW			1	1							3		1			
WWW							1		1							1
Z													2			
FF		1			1											

TABLE B.5. LSF 1H Signs

	Ts	Away									Contral			Down		Ipsil		Rear	
			-Contral	-Down	-Ipsil	-Up	-Contral Down	-Contral Up	-Down Ipsil	-Ipsil Up		-Down	-Down -Up		-Ipsil		-Up		Up
S	59 (56)	32 (20)	1	31 (13)	15 (2)	4 (1)	3	1	1	9	16 (7)	6	1	30 (24)	4 (1)	27 (4)	1	3 (1)	7 (4)
H											1	3		6		4			
HH					1									1		1			
~HH		1								3									
W		1														1			
WW				1										2					
WWW				1															
ZZ		1												2					
IF														3					

161

TABLE B.6. Auslan 1H Signs

	Ts		Away					Contral			Down		Ipsil		Rear	Up
			-Contral	-Down	-Ipsil	-Up	-Contral Down		-Down	-Up		-Ipsil		-Up		
S	63 (78)	70 (14)	2	38 (5)	4	9 (2)	1	17 (1)	5 (1)	1	58 (29)	9	35 (3)	5 (1)	6 (4)	20 (10)
H		1						3			3	1				1
HH	1					0 (1)							5			
Jab		1														
WW		2		1				1 (1)			2 (1)	1	3			
WWW							1									
Z											4				1	
ZZ		2		3							2	1	1			
IF																1
FF				1							1					1

TABLE B.7. ISN 1H Signs

	Ts		Away					Contral		Down		Ipsil		Rear	Up
			– Down	– Ipsil	– Up	– Down Ipsil	– Ipsil Up		– Down		– Ipsil		– Up		
S	29 (15)	13 (3)	16 (5)	3	2	1	2	5 (1)	4 (1)	24 (8)	3	19 (1)	4 (1)	4 (1)	8 (1)
H		2							1	4		2		1	1
HH		4								1		3		1	
WW	2	1	2							3		4		1	
WWW		1	1						1	1					
Z			2						2	1					1
ZZ										2					
FF										1*		1**			
+	2														

TABLE B.8. ASL 2HIB Signs

	Tb	OnB	PastB	Ts	Away			Down		Ipsil		Up	Rear Up
						–Ipsil	–Up		–Ipsil		–Up		
S	75 (65)	83	19 (1)	6	19 (3)	1	2	21 (3)	2 (1)	10	4	12 (2)	1
H	2	15											
HH	9	6	1		1								
Jab		1		1									
W								1				2	
IF	11												

TABLE B.9. BSL 2HIB Signs

	Tb	OnB	PastB	Ts	Away				Contral		Down		Ipsil		Up
						–Down	–Up	–Down Ipsil		–Down		–Ipsil		–Up	
S	110 (67)	81	20 (6)	9 (1)	10 (3)	2	6	2	3	1	6 (3)	1	5	3	11 (1)
Jab	7	2													
H		4													
HH				1											
Z					1										
IF	6														

TABLE B.10. LIS 2HIB Signs

	Tb	OnB	PastB	Ts		Away				Down		Ipsil		Up
						-Ipsil	-Up	-Down Ipsil	-Ipsil Up		-Ipsil		-Up	
S	40 (42)	21	8 (5)	0 (1)	7	4 (3)	1	1	4	0 (2)	1	4	9 (1)	9 (3)
H		1										1		
HH	1													
W			1											
WW	1													
Z	2													
ZZ	1													
IF	1													1

165

TABLE B.11. LSF 2HIB Signs

	Tb	OnB	PastB	Ts		Away					Down		Ipsil		Rear	Up
						−Contral	−Down	−Ipsil	−Up	−Down Ipsil		−Ipsil		−Up		
S	52 (62)	49	31 (6)	5 (9)	7 (2)	1	2	1	4 (1)	2	5 (5)	1	4 (1)	5 (2)	1	10 (3)
H		1	1		1					1	1					
HH	7	5						2		1			2			
jab	1															
W	1										1					
WW		2								1	1		2			
WWW				1	1							1				
Z				1	1											
IF	3															
FF		1														

TABLE B.12. Auslan 2HIB Signs

	Tb	OnB	PastB	Ts	Away					Down			Ipsil		Up	Rear Up
						−Down	−Ipsil	−Up	−Down Ipsil		−Contral	−Ipsil		−Up		
S	109 (61)	154	26	9 (2)	18 (2)	5	2	2	4	7 (1)	1		12	2	25 (3)	
H		6														1
HH		7			3											
jab	15															
WW		4										1				
ZZ		2			1				1							

167

TABLE B.13. ISN 2HIB

	Tb	OnB	PastB	Ts	Away		Down			Ipsil		Up
						-Down		-Contral	-Ipsil		-Up	
S	32 (25)	16 (10)	15 (8)	7	5	1	6 (1)	1		4	4	13 (1)
H		1			1					1		
HH		9								2		
W		3										
WW	1	2							1			
WWW	3								1			
Z									1			
ZZ		3										
+		1										

168

TABLE B.14. ASL 2HRM Signs

	Away						Back			Contral			Down		Ipsil		Rear	Up
		–Down	–Ipsil	–Up	–Contral Down	–Down Ipsil		–Down	–Up		–Down	–Up		–Ipsil		–Up		
S	23 (8)	15 (2)	4	3 (2)	2	10	12 (6)	2	4	11 (30)	5	2	24 (6)	3	40 (4)	7	1	11 (4)
45L	1								2									
45R				2														1
G		2				1	3 (1)						2					
G+HH	2																	
H													2					
HH	6														3			
jab										1								
WW	1			1									2		6			

169

TABLE B.15. BSL 2HRM Signs

	Away							Back				Contral			Down		Ipsil		Up
		-Contral	-Down	-Ipsil	-Up	-Contral Down	-Down Ipsil		-Down	-Up	-Contral Up		-Down	-Up		-Ipsil		-Up	
S	58(7)	3	17(8)	8	2(2)	1	3	12(4)	1(2)	5(2)	1	24(17)	11	4	31(16)	10(2)	51(3)	9	17(3)
45L		1	0(1)																
45R	1																		
G	5(1)		2				1	2											
G+45L	1		1(2)					1	1										
H															3				
HH															1		3		
WW	3																1		
ZZ																	1		

TABLE B.16. LIS 2HRM Signs

	Away									Back			Contral			Down		Ipsil		Up
		−Contral	−Down	−Ipsil	−Up	−Contral Down	−Contral Up	−Down Ipsil	−Ipsil Up		−Contral	−Down		−Down	−Up		−Ipsil		−Up	
S	8 (8)	1	15 (8)	7 (3)	1	1	1	4	1	6 (2)	4 (2)		9 (21)	6	2	24 (16)	5	25 (4)	11 (1)	7 (1)
45L	1		0 (1)		1															
45R												0 (1)				0 (1)				
G			0 (1)								1									
G+HH				1										1						
G+45L	0 (1)																			
H																3				
HH																		1		
W																4		1	1	
WW																1				
Z	1																			

171

TABLE B.17. LSF 2HRM Signs

	Away								Back				Contral			Down		Ipsl		Up
		−Contral	−Down	−Ipsil	−Up	−Contral Down	−Down Ipsil	−Ipsil Up		−Contral	−Down	−Up		−Down	−Up		−Ipsl		−Up	
S	24 (17)	1 (1)	8 (81)	8	1	7	8 (4)	2 (1)	5 (9)	1	1 (1)	3	19 (26)	8 (1)	2	29 (17)	10	27 (4)	14 (2)	13 (4)
45L	2 (1)		0 (1)						1											
45R	2 (5)		1						1				1 (1)			0 (1)				1
G	2 (4)		3 (1)	1					3 (2)			1	1			2 (1)				1
G+45L	3 (1)		1																	
H														1		4				1
HH	1													1		3				
W		1							1							3		2		2
WW																2		3	2	
IF													1		1	2		2		3
IF+45R								1												
FF																1		1		1
IF																				
ZZ																2		1		2

172

TABLE B.18. Auslan 2HRM Signs

	Away							Back				Contral			Down		Ipsil		Up
		-Contral	-Down	-Ipsil	-Up	-Down Ipsil	-Ipsil Up		-Up	-Contral Down	-Ipsil Up		-Down	-Up		-Ipsil		-Up	
S	57 (24)	0 (1)	11 (3)	12	3 (4)	9 (1)	3	9 (13)	7 (1)	1	1	28 (4)	9 (1)	4 (1)	42 (22)	9 (1)	73 (3)	13	21 (5)
45L	1		0 (1)																
45R												1							
G	3 (4)	1	1 (1)					1							1				1
G + HH	1																		
G + 45R			1 (2)																
H	1														2		1		1
HH															2		1		
WW															1				
WWW						2									1				
Z															1				
ZZ															1		1	1	
IF			1																
FF													1						

173

TABLE B.19. ISN 2HRM Signs

	Away				Back	Contral			Down		Ipsil		Up
		−Down	−Up	−Down Ipsil			−Down	−Up		−Ipsil		−Up	
S	6 (4)	3		3	3 (2)	8 (7)	5 (1)		14 (5)	2	28	21	7 (3)
45L + G					(1)				1				
45R + HH	1												
G	(1)							1					
G + WWW	(1)												
H									2				
HH	2											1	
W	4	1		1									
WW			1										
WWW					1								
Z							3			3	1		1
Z + 45L + G									2				
ZZ									2				
IF													1*

APPENDIX B

Reflexive Symmetry over Time

There are several types of signs that exhibit reflexive symmetry over time.

One type is to do something with both hands on the ipsilateral side and then on the contralateral side. Within that type, you can move both hands in the same way, as though you were doing a 2HRM sign first with the plane rotated 45° to the right, then with it rotated 45° to the left (ChSi 2HRM), or you can move only one hand with the other as a base (ChSi 2HIB).

Another type is to do something with one hand, then do it with the other. Within this type you can move the hands in the reflexive position across the plane from each other (Alt 1H), or you can glide each time (Alt 1H glide).

All six languages exhibit all these types, as seen in table B.20. For table B.20 we have two notes:

Note 1. Three signs exhibiting reflexivity over time in ISN do not appear in the table, two of them because they are polysyllabic and one because the nondominant hand acts as a fixed referent rather than a base for the dominant hand—and thus these types of signs are not part of our statistical study.

Note 2. The only ChSi 2HRM sign in ISN is actually a 2H-trans, done first on one side of the Mid plane, then on the other side, so that the overall sign is reflexive across the Mid plane.

In BSL, LSF, and Auslan, alternating signs exhibiting reflexive symmetry over time often involve multiple repetition. In table B.21 through B.23 we see the numbers of such signs for these languages

TABLE B.20. Signs Exhibiting Reflexive Symmetry over Time

	ASL	BSL	LIS	LSF	Auslan	ISN
ChSi 2HRM	2	5	2	5	3	1
ChSi 2HIB	5	2	3	2	2	4
Alt 1H	1	11		10	3	4
Alt 1H Glide	5	5	1	9	11	4

broken down by two repetitions (first one hand, then the other—as in all the alternating signs in ASL and LIS), three repetitions (the dominant hand, then the nondominant, then the dominant), four repetitions, and an indefinite number of repetitions.

With respect to table B.23, one note must be made. On the ChSi 2HRM that moves four times, the hands are glided and they come toward each other (the top one moving **Down**, the bottom one moving **Up**), then change places and do it again, then repeat the sequence. So their movement is inverted.

Table B.24 gives a summary of the data presented in the tables in appendices A and B.

TABLE B.21. BSL Breakdown of Alternating Reflexive over Time Signs by Repetition Number

	ChSi 2HRM	ChSi 2HIB	Alt 1H	Alt 1H Glide
2	5	2	1	
3				1
4			10	4

TABLE B.22. LSF Breakdown of Alternating Reflexive over Time Signs by Repetition Number

	ChSi 2HRM	ChSi 2HIB	Alt 1H	Alt 1H Glide
2	5	2	1	1
3			5	7
4			4	
Indefinite				1

TABLE B.23. Auslan Breakdown of Alternating Reflexive over Time Signs by Repetition Number

	ChSi 2HRM	ChSi 2HIB	Alt 1H	Alt 1H Glide
2	2	2	2	1
3				3
4	1		1	7

TABLE B.24. Summary Table for Data Presented in Appendices A and B

	1H	1H Swing	2HIB	2HIB Swing	2HRM	2HRM Swing	2HRM Over time	Odd Phono app. A	Poly Syll	Total
ASL	366	1	379	3	283	35	13	1	4	1,085
BSL	442	3	372	1	366	51	23	2	26	1,286
LIS	300	2	176	1	226	39	6		1	751
LSF	417	11	308		369	59	26		12	1,202
Auslan	539	27	486		434	94+3	19		16	1,618
Subtotal	2,064	44	1,721	5	1,678	278+3	87	3	59	5,942
ISN	223	14	179	4	153	40	13	11	10	647
Total	2,287	58	1,900	9	1,831	318+3	100	14	69	6,589

Appendix C
Raw Data Included in the Diagrams and Charts in the Main Text for Curve Paths for 1H, 2HIB, and 2HRM

Data on curve path signs for 1H (tables C.1 through C.6), 2HIB (tables C.7 through C.12), and 2HRM (tables C.13 through C.18) are given here.

Although in our analyses in the text we separated our signs into curve paths and noncurve paths only, when we first cataloged the signs we kept track of certain path characteristics. In the interests of others who might want to mine these data, we note these characteristics in the tables of this appendix. The symbols we used for the curve path characteristics are as follows:

arc—anywhere from about 120° to less than 360°

contact arc—make contact with the body, brushing along, and then leaving it forming an arc

circle—at least 360°

flat circle—circle with one flat side—either start straight then circle back on yourself or make a circle then go straight to the starting point for the last part of it

loop—one or more circles moving along a path

tR or tL—the curve is seen on a Mid plane tilted slightly to R or L

45R or 45L—the curve is seen on a Mid plane rotated 45° to R or L

APPENDIX C

TABLE C.1. ASL 1H Curve Signs

	CW Arc	CCW Arc	CW Loop	CW Circle	CCW Circle
HZ	2	1		1	7
VW				4	14
Mid	2	1	6	10	2

TABLE C.2. BSL 1H Curve Signs

	CW Arc	CW Contact Arc	CCW Contact Arc	CW Loop	CW Circle	CCW Circle
HZ				1	5	6
VW	1			5	4	16
Mid		2	1		8	2

TABLE C.3. LIS 1H Curve Signs

	CW Arc	CCW Arc	CW Circle	CCW Circle
HZ	3	3	5	10
VW	1	1	4	17
Mid	6	5	22	8

TABLE C.4. LSF 1H Curve Signs

	CW Arc	CCW Arc	CW Contact Arc	CW Loop	CCW Loop	CW Circle	CCW Circle
HZ	1	1		1	1	5	8
VW		1				11	8
Mid	4		2	3	2	18	18

TABLE C.5. Auslan 1H Curve Signs

	CW Arc	CCW Arc	CW Loop	CCW Loop	CW Circle	CCW Circle
HZ					9	14
VW	2	1		1		22
Mid			9		23	

TABLE C.6. ISN 1H Curve Signs

	CW Arc	CCW Arc	CW Loop	CCW Loop	CW Circle	CCW Circle
HZ	2	2			1	2
VW	1	1		1	8	
Mid	1	2	4		1	

TABLE C.7. ASL 2HIB Curve Signs

	CW Arc	CCW Arc	CW Loop	CCW Loop	CW Circle	CCW Circle
HZ		5	1	1	1	8
VW		2			2	1
Mid	3	3	1		8	

TABLE C.8. BSL 2HIB Curve Signs

	CW Arc	CCW Arc	CW Loop	CW Circle	CCW Circle
HZ	1	1		8	17
VW	1	1		2	1
Mid	4		1	6	3

TABLE C.9. LIS 2HIB Curve Signs

	CW Arc	CCW Arc	CW Loop	CCW Circle
HZ	1	1	3	7
VW			1	
Mid	9	1	9	2
tR			2	
45L			1	

TABLE C.10. LSF 2HIB Curve Signs

	CW Arc	CCW Arc	CW Loop	CW Circle	CCW Circle
HZ	1	2		9	8
VW		1		4	5
Mid	3	1	1	16	5

TABLE C.11. Auslan 2HIB Curve Signs

	CW Arc	CCW Arc	CW Loop	CCW Loop	CW Circle	CCW Circle
HZ					21	16
VW	2		1	1	3	2
Mid			3		15	1

TABLE C.12. ISN 2HIB Curve Signs

	CW Loop	CCW Loop	CW Circle	CCW Circle
HZ				6
VW	1	1		
Mid			1	

TABLE C.13. ASL 2HRM Curve Signs

	CW Arc	CCW Arc	CW Loop	CCW Loop	CW Circle	CCW Circle
HZ	3				1	9
VW		6	2	3	3	
+glid						2
Mid		1				
+inv			1	1	12	10

TABLE C.14. BSL 2HRM Curve Signs

	CW Arc	CCW Arc	CW Contact Arc	CW Loop	CW Circle	CCW Circle	CW Flat Circle	CCW Flat Circle
HZ	1	1			3	3		
+inv						1		
VW	6	4		1	2	3	1	
+inv					1	2		
Mid	1	2	1		5	1	1	1
+inv				3	21	7		

TABLE C.15. LIS 2HRM Curve Signs

	CW Arc	CCW Arc	CW Loop	CCW Loop	CW Circle	CCW Circle
HZ		6			4	1
+inv	1					
VW	11			1	3	3
+glide						1
Mid	3	4			9	1
+inv					16	4
+glide			1			
tL					1	
+inv					2	
tR +inv					2	

TABLE C.16. LSF 2HRM Curve Signs

	CW Arc	CCW Arc	CCW Loop	CW Circle	CCW Circle
HZ	1	3	1	2	1
+inv				1	2
45R				1	
VW	3	1		9	3
+glide+inv				1	
Mid	1			2	4
+inv				21	4
+glide				1	1
45R+inv				1	
45R+glide				2	
45R+glide				1	
45R+glide +inv				1	

TABLE C.17. Auslan 2HRM Curve Signs

	CW Arc	CCW Arc	CW Loop	CCW Loop	CW Circle	CCW Circle
HZ		2		1	1	6
VW	2	5	3	1	3	7
+inv	1					
Mid	1		1		4	3
+inv					19	2
+glide					1	
+inv						1
+glide					2	

TABLE C.18. ISN 2HRM Curve Signs

	CW Arc	CCW Arc	CW Loop	CCW Loop	CW Circle	CCW Circle
HZ	1	6		1		
VW	1	2		1		
+inv	1					
Mid					1	2
+inv			1			1

With respect to 2HIB curve signs across all six languages, we note the following:

Note 1. Usually arcs start at the base hand and move away from it.

Note 2. Usually circles are made close to (and sometimes touching) the base, drawing in the air beside, above, or around the base.

With respect to table C.18, one of the CW circles visible on the Mid plane involves symmetry over time.

Tables C.19 through C.21 give the summary information for curve path signs, breaking them down by 1H, 2HIB, and 2HRM. Table C.22 gives the summary information for all curve path signs noted in this appendix.

TABLE C.19. Summary Tables for 1H Curve Signs CW/CCW in Appendix C

	ASL	BSL	LIS	LSF	Auslan	Subtotal	ISN	Total
HZ	2/8	6/6	8/13	7/10	9/14	83	3/4	90
VW	4/14	10/16	5/18	11/9	2/24	113	9/2	124
Mid	18/3	10/3	28/13	27/20	32/0	154	6/2	162
Total	49	51	85	84	81	350	26	376

TABLE C.20. Summary Tables for 2HIB Curve Signs CW/CCW in Appendix C

	ASL	BSL	LIS	LSF	Auslan	Subtotal	ISN	Total
HZ	2/14	9/18	4/8	10/10	21/16	112	/6	118
VW	2/3	3/2	2/0	4/6	6/3	31	1/1	33
Mid	12/3	11/3	21/3	20/6	18/1	98	1	99
Total	36	46	38	56	65	241	9	250

TABLE C.21. Summary Tables for 2HRM Curve Signs CW/CCW in Appendix C

	ASL	BSL	LIS	LSF	Auslan	Subtotal	ISN	Total
HZ	4/9	4/5	5/7	6/6	1/8	55	1/7	63
VW	4/11	11/10	14/4	13/4	9/13	93	2/3	98
Mid	13/12	32/11	34/10	30/5	26/6	179	3/2	184
Total	53	73	74	64	63	327	18	345

TABLE C.22. Summary Tables for Signs in Appendix C

	ASL	BSL	LIS	LSF	Auslan	Subtotal	ISN	Total
1H	49	51	85	84	81	350	26	376
2HIB	36	46	38	56	65	241	9	250
2HRM	53	73	74	64	63	327	18	345
Total	138	170	197	204	209	918	53	971

Appendix D
Raw Data for the Rest
of the 2H Signs

Symmetry across Planes Other Than the Midsaggital

In table D.1, we find the number of 2HRVW noncurve signs; in table D.2, the number of 2HRHZ noncurve signs; in table D.3, the number of 2HRVW curve signs; and in table D.4, the number of 2HRHZ curve signs.

Table D.1, involving 2HRVW for noncurves, has one note: Although ISN has no 2HRVW signs with primary movement, it does have one such sign that has only secondary movement (and is also +glide).

The tables involving 2HRHZ call for notes.

With regard to table D.2, we have three notes:

Note 1. BSL: The **Contral** sign is glided and the HZ plane is slightly tilted so the right side is higher.

Note 2. LIS: One of the **Up** signs has the HZ plane slightly tilted so the left side is higher.

Note 3. Auslan: The **Contral** sign is glided. Not included on the table is a horizontal swing **Away-Back** with glide and inversion (EGYPT).

TABLE D.1. 2HRVW for Noncurves

	A	B
ASL	5	
BSL	2	
LIS		
LSF	2	1
Auslan	1	
ISN		

APPENDIX D

TABLE D.2. 2HRHZ for Noncurves

	A	−D	B	C	D	I	U	C-I Swing
ASL	2				3	1		
BSL	2			1	2		1	
LIS							2	
LSF			1	1	3		2	
Auslan	1		3	1	3		2	
ISN	1				1		1	1

TABLE D.3. 2HRVW for Curves

	CW Circle
ASL	
BSL	
LIS	
LSF	
Auslan	1
ISN	

TABLE D.4. 2HRHZ for Curves

	CW Loop	CCW Loop	CW Circle	CCW Circle
ASL	1	1	2	4
BSL				3
LIS				3
LSF			1	1
Auslan			7	
ISN				

With regard to table D.4, we have four notes:

Note 1. The ASL and BSL CCW circles have inversion.

Note 2. The LIS CCW circles deserve special mention. In one the hands are connected, so they move in a single circle as a unit. Additionally, one of these signs is glided.

Note 3. The LSF CCW circle has inversion.

Note 4. All the CW circles have inversion, and one of the Auslan circles is glided.

Rotational Symmetry (2H-Rot)

The data are shown in table D.5. Note that one of the LSF 2H-rot with respect to the VW plane is glided, and one each of the ASL and Auslan 2H-rot with respect to the HZ plane is glided.

Translation Symmetry (2H-Trans)

The total number of 2H-trans signs that are swings are given in table D.6. All signs that have the hands connected are tallied after a "/" within a given table cell. Note that the 2H-trans swings differ from 2HRM **Contral-Ipsil** swings in that both hands move **Contral**, then both move **Ipsil**, and so on, whereas with the 2HRM **Contral-Ipsil** swings, both hands move away from the plane then toward the plane, and so on.

TABLE D.5. Rotational Symmetry

	ASL	BSL	LIS	LSF	Auslan	ISN
Mid	6	3	1	1	4	0
HZ	5	4	3	1	2	1
VW	5	2	1	3	1	0

TABLE D.6. Translation Swings: Separated Hands/Connected Hands

	C-I	I-U
ASL	14	
BSL	2/3	
LIS	4	
LSF	2	
Auslan	3	
ISN	3	1

In table D.7 we see the tallies for 2H-trans signs that are not swings and have noncurve paths. The column shows the direction both hands move. If the direction is **Contral** or **Ipsil** (or a slight combination of one of them with another direction), the path could be any shape. But if the direction is anything else, we either specify the path shape (WW, WWW, or ZZ) or indicate that the hands have an orientation (Orient) that shows this movement is translation and not reflexivity. This table is for noncurve paths.

TABLE D.7. 2H-Trans Noncurve Paths, Separate Hands/Connected Hands

		Contral					
	Away	$-$Down	$-$Up		Ipsil	Down	Up
ASL		2/0			4/1	1[a]	
BSL	1[c]	3/0			3/1	1[b]/2[d]	
LIS	1[a]		1		4		
LSF		2/1			7/3		
Auslan	1[c]				5/2	0/2[d]	0/1[d]
	1[a]	3/1					
ISN		1	/1	1	/1		

a = WW
b = WWW
c = ZZ
d = Orient

There are two notes to make with respect to table D.7:

Note 1. ASL: One of the **Ipsil** translations has a ZZ path with inversion.

Note 2. Auslan: Not included is one translation over time (first the dominant hand, then the nondominant).

In table D.8 we see the tallies for 2H-trans signs that are not swings and have curve paths.

Summary Tables

Table D.9 gives a summary of the signs of this appendix.
Table D.10 gives a summary of the signs of all appendices.

TABLE D.8. 2H-Trans Curve Paths, Separate Hands/Connected Hands

	CCW Arc VW	CW Loop HZ	CW Circle HZ	CW Circle VW	CW Circle VW +inv	CCW Circle HZ
ASL		2	3/4			
BSL	1		1/5	1/0		0/1
LIS						
LSF			1		1	1
Auslan			0/4			0/4
ISN				/1		

TABLE D.9. Summary of Symmetries Other Than 2HRM

	Sym VW	Sym HZ	Rotation	Translation	Total
ASL	5	14	16	31	66
BSL	2	9	9	25	45
LIS	0	5	5	10	20
LSF	3	9	5	18	35
Auslan	1	16+1	7	27+1	53
ISN	0	4	1	9	14

TABLE D.10. Summary Table for All Primary Movement Signs in All Appendices

	ASL	BSL	LIS	LSF	Auslan	Subtotal	ISN	Total
Noncurve primary movement: appendices A and B	1,085	1,286	751	1,202	1,618	5,942	647	6,589
Curve primary movement: appendix C	138	170	197	204	209	918	53	971
Symmetries other than 2HRM: appendix D	66	45	20	35	53	219	14	235
Total	1,289	1,501	968	1,441	1,880	7,079	714	7,793

APPENDIX E
RESOURCES ON ADDITIONAL SIGN LANGUAGES

We list these alphabetically, according to the contact spoken language, on the assumption that our readers are more likely to know the name of the contact spoken language than of the sign language.

Catalan. Approximately 800 entries: http://lsc.wikisign.org/wiki/Especial:Allpages

Czech. Two volumes (2002–2004), A–N and O–Z: http://knihy.heureka.cz/vseobecny-slovnik-ceskeho-znakoveho-jazyka-a-n/
http://knihy.heureka.cz/vseobecny-slovnik-ceskeho-znakoveho-jazyka-o-z/

Indo-Pakistani. Several books on this website are dictionaries: http://www.southasiabibliography.de/Bibliography/Sign_Languages__All_Dialects_/sign_languages__all_dialects_.html

Japanese. Multivolume set: http://translate.googleusercontent.com/translate_c?hl=en&ie=UTF-8&sl=ja&tl=en&u=http://jfd.shop-pro.jp/%3Fpid%3D18441018&prev=_t&rurl=translate.google.com&usg=ALkJrhgliB84cb_UfPLEqv6ZYhqtgZQB_A (Note: In addition, a Japanese Sign Language dictionary with English translations was published in an extremely limited number for use in 1997 when the Japanese Federation for the Deaf hosted the World Federation for the Deaf Conference in Tokyo.)

Hong Kong. http://www.chineseupress.com/asp/e_Book_card.asp?BookID=2029&Lang=E

Nepali. 1,500 entries, compiled in 1995, with English glosses: http://dl.dropbox.com/u/2420238/nsld.pdf

Spanish. 3,600 entries: http://fundacioncnse.org/eleboracion .html

Vietnamese. Two volumes (84 pp, 79 pp); *Ho Chi Minh City Sign Language Dictionary.* Available through Gallaudet University Library via interlibrary loan: http://aquadev.wrlc.org/?skin=ga &q=Ho+Chi+Minh+City+Sign+Language+Dictionary

Huge resources are also available through "SignPuddle," connected to the Sutton Sign Writing project. Enter an asterisk (*) in the field that comes up, and hit return. The total number of recorded signs for each language listed below is shown in parentheses. "w. Eng" indicates that English glosses are given.

American (8,239): http://www.signbank.org/SignPuddle1.5 /searchword.php?ui=1&sgn=4

Argentine (672): http://www.signbank.org/SignPuddle1.5 /searchword.php?ui=5&sgn=41

Belgian (1,516): http://www.signbank.org/SignPuddle1.5 /searchword.php?ui=4&sgn=43

Catalan (2,949): http://www.signbank.org/SignPuddle1.5 /searchword.php?ui=3&sgn=56

Czech (1,663, w. Eng): http://www.signbank.org /SignPuddle1.5/searchword.php?ui=6&sgn=52

Flemish (4,349, w. Eng): http://www.signbank.org /SignPuddle1.5/searchword.php?ui=1&sgn=44

French (1,201): http://www.signbank.org/SignPuddle1.5 /searchword.php?ui=4&sgn=58

French (Swiss) (4,797, with video): http://www.signbank. org/SignPuddle1.5/searchword.php?ui=4&sgn=49

German (12,389): http://www.signbank.org/SignPuddle1.5 /searchword.php?ui=3&sgn=53

Japanese (153): http://www.signbank.org/SignPuddle1.5 /searchword.php?ui=1&sgn=64

Maltese (531, w. English): http://www.signbank.org /SignPuddle1.5/searchword.php?ui=1&sgn=31

Nicaraguan (893): http://www.signbank.org/SignPuddle1.5
/searchword.php?ui=5&sgn=67
Norwegian (1,360): http://www.signbank.org/SignPuddle1.5
/searchword.php?ui=3&sgn=69
Philippines (854): http://www.signbank.org/SignPuddle1.5
/searchword.php?ui=1&sgn=72
Polish (2,094, w. Eng): http://www.signbank.org
/SignPuddle1.5/searchword.php?ui=7&sgn=19
Spanish (7,546): http://www.signbank.org/SignPuddle1.5
/searchword.php?ui=5&sgn=55

In addition, we note that Tibetan Sign Language is slated to be covered in a three-volume dictionary when the Tibet Deaf Association (tibetdeaf@gmail.com) secures funding. Also, Taiwanese Sign Language offers a limited online video dictionary (http://tsl.ccu .edu.tw), but a printed form is yet to come (though it is promised). Finally, see the listings in Carmel (1992).

BIBLIOGRAPHY

Ajello, Roberto, Laura Mazzoni, and Florida Nicolai. 2001. Mouthing in Italian Sign Language (LIS). In *The hands are the head of the mouth. The mouth as articulator in sign languages* (International Studies on Sign Language and Communication of the Deaf 39), eds. Penny Boyes-Braem and Rachel Sutton-Spence, 231–46. Hamburg: Signum-Verlag.

Baker-Shenk, Charlotte L., and Dennis Cokely. 1991. *American sign language: A teacher's resource text on grammar and culture*. 4th ed. Washington, DC: Gallaudet University Press.

Battison, Robert. 1974. Phonological deletion in American Sign Language. *Sign Language Studies* 5:1019.

Battison, Robert. 1978. *Lexical borrowing in American Sign Language*. Silver Spring, MD: Linstok Press.

Bernal, Brian, and Lyn Wilson. 2004. *Dictionary of Auslan: English to Auslan*. Melbourne: Deaf Children Australia.

Blondel, Marion, and Christopher Miller. 2000. Rhythmic structures in French Sign Language (LSF) nursery rhymes. *Sign Language and Linguistics* 3 (1): 79–100.

Blondel, Marion, and Christopher Miller. 2001. Movement and rhythm in nursery rhymes in LSF. *Sign Language Studies* 2 (1): 24–61.

Bornstein, Harry. 1990. *Manual communication: Implications for education*. Washington, DC: Gallaudet University Press.

Boula de Mareüil, Philippe, Giovanna Marotta, and Martine Adda-Decker. 2004. Contribution of prosody to the perception of Spanish/Italian accents. Paper presented at Speech Prosody 2004, Nara, Japan, 681–84.

Boyes-Braem, Penny. 1990. Acquisition of the handshape in American Sign Language: A preliminary analysis. In *From gesture to language in hearing and deaf children*, eds. Virginia Volterra and Carol J. Erting, 107–27. Heidelberg: Springer-Verlag.

Boyes-Braem, Penny, and Rachel Sutton-Spence, eds. 2001. *The hands are the head of the mouth: The mouth as articulator in sign languages* (International Studies on Sign Language and Communication of the Deaf 39). Hamburg: Signum-Verlag.

BIBLIOGRAPHY

Brennan, Mary. 1990. *Word-formation in British Sign Language.* Stockholm: Stockholm University Press.

Brennan, Mary. 2001. Making borrowings work in British Sign Language. In *Foreign vocabulary in sign languages: A cross-linguistic investigation of sign languages,* ed. Diane Brentari, 49–85. Mahwah, NJ: Lawrence Erlbaum.

Brennan, Mary, and Graham Turner, eds. 1994. *Word-order issues in sign language.* Durham, UK: International Sign Linguistics Association.

Brentari, Diane. 1990. Theoretical foundations of American Sign Language phonology. PhD diss., University of Chicago.

Brentari, Diane. 1998. *A prosodic model of sign language phonology.* Cambridge, MA: MIT Press.

Brentari, Diane. 2001. Borrowed elements in sign languages: A window on word formation. In *Foreign vocabulary in sign languages: A cross-linguistic investigation of sign languages,* ed. Diane Brentari, ix–xx. Mahwah, NJ: Lawrence Erlbaum.

Brentari, Diane, and Carol Padden. 2001. Native and foreign vocabulary in American Sign Language: A lexicon with multiple origins. In *Foreign vocabulary in sign languages: A cross-linguistic investigation of sign languages,* ed. Diane Brentari, 87–119. Mahwah, NJ: Lawrence Erlbaum.

Brien, David. 1992. *Dictionary of British Sign Language/English.* London: Faber and Faber.

Burleson, Deborah F. 2007. Improving intelligibility of non-native speech with computer-assisted phonological training. Indiana University Linguistics Club Working Papers Online, https://www.indiana.edu/~iulcwp/pdfs/07-Burleson5.pdf (accessed March 23, 2009).

Butcher, Cynthia, Carolyn Mylander, and Susan Goldin-Meadow. 1991. Displaced communication in a self-styled gesture system: Pointing at the non-present. *Cognitive Development* 6:315–42.

Carmel, Simon. 1992. A checklist of dictionaries of national sign languages of Deaf people. *Sign Language Studies* 76:233–52.

Chen, Si-Qing. 1990. A study of communication strategies in interlanguage production by Chinese EFL learners. *Language Learning* 40 (2): 155–87.

Cienki, Alan, and Cornelia Müller, eds. 2008. *Metaphor and gesture.* (Gesture studies 3). Amsterdam: John Benjamins.

Coerts, Jane. 1994. Constituent order in Sign Language of the Netherlands. In *Word-order issues in sign language,* eds. Mary Brennan and Graham Turner, 47–70. Durham, UK: International Sign Linguistics Association.

Corina, David. 1990a. Handshape assimilation in hierarchical phonological representations. In *Sign language research: Theoretical issues,* ed. Ceil Lucas, 27–49. Washington, DC: Gallaudet University Press.

BIBLIOGRAPHY

Corina, David. 1990b. Reassessing the role of sonority in syllable structure: Evidence from a visual-gestural language. *Papers from the Chicago Linguistics Society* 26 (2): 33–44.

Corina, David, and Ursula Hildebrandt. 2002. Psycholinguistic investigations of phonological structure in ASL. In *Modality and structure in signed and spoken languages*, eds. Richard P. Meier, Kearsy Cormier, and David Quinto-Pozos, 88–111. Cambridge: Cambridge University Press.

Costello, Elaine. 1994. *Random House American Sign Language dictionary*. New York: Random House.

Crowley, Terry. 1992. *An introduction to historical linguistics*. 2nd ed. Auckland: Oxford University Press.

de Jorio, Andrea. 1832. *La mimica degli antichi investigata nel gestire napoletano*. Naples: Stamperia e Cartiera del Fibreno.

De Lange, Olivier, Pierre Guitteny, Henri Portine, and Christian Retoré. 2004. A propos des structures OSV en langue des signes française. *Silexicales* 4:115–30.

Deuchar, Margaret. 1978. Sign language diglossia in a British Deaf community. *Sign Language Studies* 17:347–56.

Deuchar, Margaret. 1983. Is BSL an SOV language? In *Language in sign: An international perspective on sign language*, eds. Jim Kyle and Bencie Woll, 59–76. London: Croom Helm.

Duncan, Susan D. 1996. Grammatical form and 'thinking-for-speaking' in Mandarin Chinese and English: An analysis based on speech-accompanying gesture. PhD diss., University of Chicago.

Duncan, Susan D. 2002. Gesture, verb aspect, and the nature of iconic imagery in natural discourse. *Gesture* 2 (2): 183–206.

Dye, Matthew, and Shui-I Shih. 2006. Phonological priming in British Sign Language. In *Laboratory phonology 8: Varieties of phonological competence*, eds. Louis Goldstein, Douglas H. Whalen, and Catherine T. Best, 241–63. Berlin: Mouton de Gruyter.

Efron, David. 1941. *Gesture and environment: A tentative study of some of the spatio-temporal and 'linguistic' aspects of the gestural behavior of eastern Jews and southern Italians in New York City, living under similar as well as different environmental conditions*. New York: King's Crown Press.

Ekman, Paul, and Wallace V. Friesen. 1969. The repertoire of non-verbal behavior: Categories, origins, usage and coding. *Semiotica* 1:49–98.

Emmorey, Karen, and Judy Reilly, eds. 1995. *Language, gesture and space*. Hillsdale, NJ: Lawrence Erlbaum.

Engberg-Pedersen, Elisabeth. 2004. From pointing to reference and predication: Pointing signs, eye gaze, and head and body orientation in Danish Sign Language. In *Pointing. Where language, culture, and cognition meet*, ed. Sotaro Kita, 269–92. Mahwah, NJ: Lawrence Erlbaum.

BIBLIOGRAPHY

Farnell, Brenda. 1995. *Do you see what I mean?: Plains Indian Sign Talk and the embodiment of action.* Austin: University of Texas Press.

Faurot, Karla, Dianne Dellinger, Andy Eatough, and Steve Parkhurst. 1999. The identity of Mexican Sign as a language, http://www.sil.org/mexico/lenguajes-de-signos/G009i-Identity-mfs.pdf (accessed February 25, 2009).

Fischer, Susan. 1975. Influences on word order change in American Sign Language. In *Word order and word order change*, ed. Charles Li, 3–25. Austin: University of Texas Press.

Flege, James E. 1987. The production of 'new' and 'similar' phones in a foreign language: Evidence for the effect of equivalence classification. *Journal of Phonetics* 15:47–65.

Frishberg, Nancy. 1975. Arbitrariness and iconicity: Historical change in American Sign Language. *Language* 51:696–719.

Goldin-Meadow, Susan. 2003. *The resilience of language: What gesture creation in deaf children can tell us about how all children learn language.* New York: Psychology Press.

Goldin-Meadow, Susan, and Carolyn Mylander. 1990. Beyond the input given: the child's role in the acquisition of language. *Language* 66 (2): 323–55.

Gomez, Juan Javier. 1997. *Diccionario del idioma de señas de Nicaragua.* Managua, Nicaragua: Asociación Nacional de Sordos de Nicaragua.

Graham, Jean Ann, and Michael Argyle. 1975. A cross-cultural study of the communication of extra-verbal meaning by gestures. *International Journal of Psychology* 10:57–67.

Graham, Jean Ann, and Simon Heywood. 1975. The effects of elimination of hand gestures and of verbal codability on speech performance. *European Journal of Social Psychology* 5 (2): 189–95.

Groce, Nora. 1985. *Everyone here spoke sign language: Hereditary deafness on Martha's Vineyard.* Cambridge, MA: Harvard University Press.

Gudschinsky, Sarah C. 1964. The *ABC's* of lexicostatistics (glottochronology). In *Language in culture and society: A reader in linguistics and anthropology*, ed. Dell Hymes, 612–23. New York: Harper and Row.

Gullberg, Marianne. 1998. *Gesture as a communication strategy in second language discourse: A study of learners of French and Swedish.* Lund, Sweden: Lund University Press.

Haviland, John B. 2000. Pointing, gesture spaces, and mental maps. In *Language and gesture: Window into thought and action*, ed. David McNeill, 13–46. Cambridge: Cambridge University Press.

Huber, Peter J. 2004. *Robust statistics.* New York: Wiley.

Iverson, Jana M., Olga Capirci, Virginia Volterra, and Susan Goldin-Meadow. 2008. Learning to talk in a gesture-rich world: Early communication in Italian vs. American children. *First Language* 28:164–81.

BIBLIOGRAPHY

Jantunen, Tommi. 2008. Fixed and free: Order of the verbal predicate and its core arguments in declarative transitive clauses in Finnish Sign Language. *SKY Journal of Linguistics* 21:83–123, http://www.linguistics.fi/julkaisut/SKY2008/Jantunen_NETTIVERSIO.pdf. (accessed February 25, 2009).

Johnston, Trevor A. 1989. Auslan: The sign language of the Australian Deaf community. PhD diss., University of Sydney.

Johnston, Trevor, and Adam Schembri. 1999. On defining lexeme in a sign language. *Sign Language and Linguistics* 2 (1): 115–85.

Johnston, Trevor, and Adam Schembri. 2007. *Australian sign language (Auslan): An introduction to sign language linguistics.* Cambridge: Cambridge University Press.

Johnston, Trevor, Myriam Vermeerbergen, Adam Schembri, and Lorraine Leeson. 2007. 'Real data are messy': Considering cross-linguistic analysis of constituent ordering in Auslan, VGT, and ISL. In *Visible variation: Comparative studies on sign language structure,* eds. Pamela Perniss, Roland Pfau, and Markus Steinbach, 163–206. Berlin: Mouton de Gruyter.

Joseph, Brian D., and Richard D. Janda, eds. 2004. *Handbook of historical linguistics.* Malden, MA: Blackwell.

Kegl, Judy, Ann Senghas, and Marie Coppola. 1999. Creation through contact: Sign language emergence and sign language change in Nicaragua. In *Language creation and language change: Creolization, diachrony, and development,* ed. Michel DeGraff, 179–237. Cambridge, MA: MIT Press.

Kendon, Adam. 1980. Gesticulation and speech: Two aspects of the process of utterance. In *Nonverbal communication and language,* ed. Mary Ritchie Key, 207–27. The Hague: Mouton de Gruyter.

Kendon, Adam. 1988. *Sign languages of Aboriginal Australia: Cultural, semiotic and communicative perspectives.* Cambridge: Cambridge University Press.

Kendon, Adam. 1995. Andrea De Jorio—the first ethnographer of gesture? *Visual Anthropology* 7:375–94.

Kendon, Adam. 2004a. Contrasts in gesticulation: A Neapolitan speaker and a British speaker compared. In *Semantics and pragmatics of everyday gestures,* eds. Cornelia Muller and Roland Posner, 173–93. Berlin: Weidler Buchverlag.

Kendon, Adam. 2004b. *Gesture: Visible action as utterance.* Cambridge: Cambridge University Press.

Kestler, Hans A., André Muller, Johann M. Kraus, Malte Buchholz, Thomas M. Gress, Hongfang Liu, David W. Kane, Barry R. Zeeberg, and John N. Weinstein. 2008. VennMaster: Area-proportional Euler diagrams for functional GO analysis of microarrays. *BMC Bioinformatics* 9 (1): 67, http://www.pubmedcentral.nih.gov/articlerender.fcgi?artid=2335321 (accessed February 25, 2009).

Kita, Sotaro. 1993. Language and thought interface: A study of spontaneous gestures and Japanese mimetics. PhD diss., University of Chicago.

Kita, Sotaro. 2000. Why do people gesture? *Cognitive Studies: Bulletin of the Japanese Cognitive Science Society* 7 (1): 9–21.

Klima, Edward, and Ursula Bellugi. 1979. *The signs of language.* Cambridge, MA: Harvard University Press.

Labov, William, Sharon Ash, and Charles Boberg. 2005. *Atlas of North American English: Phonetics, phonology and sound change.* The Hague: Mouton de Gruyter.

Lane, Harlan. 1984. *When the mind hears: A history of the deaf.* New York: Random House.

LeBaron, Curtis, and Jiirgen Streeck. 2000. Gestures, knowledge, and the world. In *Language and gesture: Window into thought and action,* ed. David McNeill, 118–38. Cambridge: Cambridge University Press.

Leeson, Lorraine. 2001. *Aspects of verbal valency in Irish Sign Language.* PhD diss., Trinity College Dublin.

Leeson, Lorraine. 2005. Vying with variation: Interpreting language contact, gender variation and generational difference. In *Topics in signed language interpreting,* ed. Terry Janzen, 251–92. Amsterdam: John Benjamins.

Lehmann, Winfred P. 1962. *Historical linguistics: An introduction.* New York: Holt, Rinehart and Winston.

Liddell, Scott. 2003. *Grammar, gesture, and meaning in American Sign Language.* Cambridge: Cambridge University Press.

Liddell, Scott K., and Robert E. Johnson. 1989. American Sign Language: The phonological base. *Sign Language Studies* 64:195–277.

Lupton, Linda, and Joe Salmons. 1996. A re-analysis of the creole status of American Sign Language. *Sign Language Studies* 90:80–94.

Machabée, Dominique, and Colette Dubuisson. 1995. Initialized signs in (or outside of?) Quebec Sign Language. In *Sign language research 1994, Proceedings of the 4th European Congress on Sign Language Research,* eds. Heleen Bos and Trude Schermer, 69–83. Hamburg: Signum-Verlag.

Mai, Mark. 2009. Phonetic diversity in internal movement across five sign languages: A study of ASL, BSL, LIS, LSF, and Auslan. Senior Thesis, Swarthmore College, http://www.swarthmore.edu/SocSci/Linguistics/xling131-2009.html (accessed December 13, 2010).

Maiden, Martin, John C. Smith, and Adam Ledgeway. 2010. *The Cambridge history of the Romance languages.* Cambridge: Cambridge University Press.

Marazzini, Claudio. 1999. *Da Dante alla lingua selvaggia. Sette secoli di dibattito sull'italiano.* Rome: Carocci.

BIBLIOGRAPHY

Matthews, Patrick. 1996. *The Irish Deaf community.* Vol. 1. Dublin: ITE.

Mayfield Tomokiyo, Laura, and Alex Waibel. 2001. Adaptation methods for non-native speech. Proceedings of Multilinguality in Spoken Language Processing, 7th European Conference on Speech Communication and Technology, Eurospeech 2001, Aalborg, Denmark, September 13, 2001, http://www.cs.cmu.edu/~laura/pages/publications.html (accessed February 25, 2009).

McDonald, Betsy. 1983. Productive and frozen lexicon in ASL: An old problem revisited. Paper presented at the 3rd International Symposium on Sign Language Research, Rome, 1983.

McDonnell, Patrick. 1996. Verb categories in Irish Sign Language. PhD diss., Trinity College Dublin.

McKee, David, and Graeme Kennedy. 2000. Lexical comparison of signs from American, Australian, British, and New Zealand sign languages. In *The signs of language revisited: An anthology in honor of Ursula Bellugi and Edward Klima,* eds. Karen Emmorey and Harlan Lane, 49–76. Mahwah, NJ: Lawrence Erlbaum.

McNeill, David. 1985. So you think gestures are nonverbal? *Psychological Review* 92:350–71.

McNeill, David. 1992. *Hand and mind.* Chicago: University of Chicago Press.

McNeill, David, ed. 2000a. Introduction. In *Language and gesture,* ed. David McNeill, 1–12. Cambridge: Cambridge University Press.

McNeill, David, ed. 2000b. *Language and gesture.* Cambridge: Cambridge University Press.

Milkovic, Marina, Sandra Bradaric-Joncic, and Ronnie Wilbur. 2007. Information status and word order in Croatian Sign Language. *Clinical Linguistics & Phonetics* 21 (11–12): 1007–17.

Miller, Christopher. 2001. The adaptation of loan words in Quebec Sign Language: Multiple sources, multiple processes. In *Foreign vocabulary in sign languages: A cross-linguistic investigation of sign languages,* ed. Diane Brentari, 139–73. Mahwah, NJ: Lawrence Erlbaum.

Moody, Bill, Agnès Vourc'h, Michel Girod, and Anne-Catherine Dufour. 1997. *La Langue des signes: Dictionnaire bilingue LSF/français.* Vols. 1 and 2. Paris: Ellipses.

Moores, Donald F. 2001. *Educating the deaf: Psychology, principles, and practices.* Boston: Houghton Mifflin.

Morford, Jill P., and Judy Kegl. 2000. Gestural precursors of linguistic constructs: How input shapes the form of language. In *Language and gesture,* ed. David McNeill, 358–87. Cambridge: Cambridge University Press.

Morford, Jill P., Jenny L. Singleton, and Susan Goldin-Meadow. 1995. The genesis of language: How much time is needed to generate arbitrary

BIBLIOGRAPHY

symbols in a sign system? In *Language, gesture, and space,* eds. Karen Emmorey and Judy S. Reilly, 313–32. Hillsdale, NJ: Lawrence Erlbaum.

Morgan, Gary. 2006. Children are just lingual: The development of phonology in British Sign Language (BSL). *Lingua* 116 (10): 1507–23, http://www.staff.city.ac.uk/g.morgan/BSL%20phonology%20lingua.pdf (accessed February 25, 2009).

Müller, Cornelia, and Roland Posner, eds. 2004. *The semantics and pragmatics of everyday gestures. The Berlin conference.* Berlin: Weidler Buchverlag.

Munro, Murray J., and Tracey M. Derwing. 1995. Foreign accent, comprehensibility, and intelligibility in the speech of second language learners. *Language Learning* 45 (1): 73–97.

Napoli, Donna Jo, and Rachel Sutton-Spence. n.d. Word order in sign languages. Swarthmore College, Department of Linguistics.

Napoli, Donna Jo, and Jeffrey Wu. 2003. Morpheme structure constraints on two-handed signs in American Sign Language: Notions of symmetry. *Sign Language and Linguistics* 6:123–205.

Nyst, Victoria. 2007. A descriptive analysis of Adamorobe Sign Language. PhD diss., University of Amsterdam.

Özyürek, Asli. 2000. The influence of addressee location on spatial language and representational gestures of direction. In *Language and gesture* (Series in language, culture and cognition 2), ed. David McNeill, 64–82. Cambridge: Cambridge University Press.

Padden, Carol. 2010. Sign language geography. In *Deaf around the world,* eds. Gaurav Mathur and Donna Jo Napoli, 21–49. Oxford: Oxford University Press.

Padden, Carol, and Tom Humphries. 1988. *Deaf in America.* Cambridge, MA: Harvard University Press.

Patrick, Peter. 1999. *Urban Jamaican Creole: Variation in the mesolect.* Amsterdam: John Benjamins.

Perlmutter, David. 1992. Sonority and syllable structure in American Sign Language. *Linguistic Inquiry* 23:407–42.

Perniss, Pamela, Roland Pfau, and Markus Steinbach, eds. 2007. *Visible variation. Comparative studies on sign language structure.* Berlin: Mouton de Gruyter.

Pika, Simone, Elena Nicoladis, and Paula Marentette. 2006. A cross-cultural study on the use of gestures: Evidence for cross-linguistic transfer? *Language and Cognition* 9:319–27.

Poizner, Howard, Ursula Bellugi, and Venita Lutes-Driscoll. 1981. Perception of American Sign Language in dynamic point-light displays. *Journal of Experimental Psychology: Human Perception and Performance* 7 (2): 430–40.

BIBLIOGRAPHY

Posner, Rebecca. 1996. *The Romance languages*. Cambridge: Cambridge University Press.

Radutzky, Elena. 1993. The education of Deaf people in Italy and the use of Italian Sign Language. In *Deaf history unveiled: Interpretations from the new scholarship*, ed. John Vickrey Van Cleve, 237–51. Washington, DC: Gallaudet University Press.

Radutzky, Elena. 2001. *Dizionario bilingue elementare della lingua italiana dei segni*. Rome: Edizioni Kappa.

Rauscher, Frances, Robert Krauss, and Yihsiu Chen. 1996. Gesture, speech and lexical access: The role of lexical movements in speech production. *Psychological Science* 7:226–31.

Ríme, Bernard, and Loris Schiaratura. 1991. Gesture and Speech. In *Fundamentals of nonverbal behavior*, eds. Robert S. Feldman and Bernard Ríme, 239–81. New York: Press Syndicate of the University of Cambridge.

Ríme, Bernard, Loris Schiaratura, Michael Hupet, and Anne Ghysselinckx. 1984. Effects of relative immobilization on the speaker's nonverbal behavior and on the dialogue imagery level. *Motivation and Emotion* 8:311–25.

Rochet, Bernard L. 1995. Perception and production of second-language speech sounds by adults. In *Speech perception and linguistic experience: Theoretical and methodological issues*, ed. Winifred Strange, 379–411. Timonium, MD: York Press.

Romeo, Orazio. 1991. *Dizionario dei segni: La lingua dei segni in 1400 immagini*. Bologna, Italy: Zanichelli.

Rousseeuw, Peter, and Annick M. Leroy. 2003. *Robust regression and outlier detection*. New York: Wiley.

Russo, Tommaso. 2004. Iconicity and productivity in sign language discourse: An analysis of three LIS discourse registers. *Sign Language Studies* 4:164–97.

Sacks, Oliver. 1989. *Seeing voices: A journey into the land of the deaf*. Berkeley: University of California Press.

Sandler, Wendy. 1986. The spreading hand autosegment of American Sign Language. *Sign Language Studies* 50:1–28.

Sandler, Wendy. 1987. Assimilation and feature hierarchy in American Sign Language. *Papers from the Chicago Linguistics Society; Parasession on Autosegmenta Phonology* 23 (2): 266–78.

Sandler, Wendy. 1989. *Phonological representation of the sign*. Dordrecht: Foris.

Sandler, Wendy. 1993. A sonority cycle in American Sign Language. *Phonology* 10 (2): 243–79.

Sandler, Wendy. 1999. Cliticization and prosodic words in a sign language. In *Studies on the phonological word*, eds. Tracy Alan Hall and Ursula Kleinhenz, 223–54. Amsterdam: John Benjamins.

BIBLIOGRAPHY

Sandler, Wendy, and Diane Carolyn Lillo-Martin. 2006. *Sign language and linguistic universals.* Cambridge: Cambridge University Press.

Schembri, Adam, and Trevor Johnston. 2004. Sociolinguistic variation in Auslan Australian Sign Language: A research project in progress. *Deaf Worlds* 201:S78–S90.

Schembri, Adam, and Trevor Johnston. 2007. Sociolinguistic variation in the use of fingerspelling in Australian Sign Language: A pilot study. *Sign Language Studies* 7 (3): 319–47.

Shumway-Cook, Anne, and Marjorie H. Woollacott. 2007. *Motor control: Translating research into clinical practice.* Philadelphia: Lippincott Williams & Wilkins.

Singleton, Jenny L., Jill P. Morford, and Susan Goldin-Meadow. 1993. Once is not enough: Standards of well-formedness in manual communication created over three different timespans. *Language* 69:683–715.

Supalla, Ted. 2004. The validity of the Gallaudet lecture films. *Sign Language Studies* 4 (3): 261–92.

Sutton-Spence, Rachel. 1994. The role of the manual alphabet and fingerspelling in BSL. PhD diss., University of Bristol.

Sutton-Spence, Rachel. 1998. Grammatical constraints on fingerspelled English verb loans in BSL. In *Pinky extension and eye gaze: Language use in Deaf communities* (Sociolinguistics in Deaf Communities 4), ed. Ceil Lucas, 41–58. Washington, DC: Gallaudet University Press.

Sutton-Spence, Rachel, and Linda Day. 2001. Mouthings and mouth gestures in British Sign Language (BSL). In *The hands are the head of the mouth: The mouth as articulator in sign language,* eds. Rachel Sutton-Spence and Penny Boyes-Braem, 69–85. Hamburg: Signum-Verlag.

Sutton-Spence, Rachel, and Bencie Woll. 1993. The status and functional role of fingerspelling in BSL. In *Psychological perspectives on deafness,* eds. Marc Marschark and M. Diane Clark, 185–207. Hillsdale, NJ: Lawrence Erlbaum.

Sutton-Spence, Rachel, and Bencie Woll. 1999. *The linguistics of British Sign Language: An introduction.* Cambridge: Cambridge University Press.

Sutton-Spence, Rachel, Bencie Woll, and Lorna Allsop. 1990. Variation and recent change in fingerspelling in British Sign Language. *Language Variation and Change* 2:313–30.

Suwanarat, Manfa, Anucha Ratanasint, Vilaiporn Rungsrithong, Lloyd Anderson, and Owen P. Wrigley. 1990. *The Thai Sign Language dictionary.* Bangkok: The National Association of the Deaf in Thailand.

Tabak, John. 2006. *Significant gestures: A history of American Sign Language.* Westport, CT: Praeger Publishers.

Taub, Sarah F. 2001. *Language from the body: Iconicity and metaphor in American Sign Language.* Cambridge: Cambridge University Press.

BIBLIOGRAPHY

Tennant, Richard A., and Marianne Gluszak Brown. 2002. *The American Sign Language handshape dictionary*. Washington, DC: Gallaudet University Press.

Umiker-Sebeok, Jean, and Thomas A. Sebeok, eds. 1987. *Monastic sign languages*. Berlin: Mouton de Gruyter.

Van Cleve, John Vickrey, and Barry A. Crouch. 1989. *A place of their own: Creating the Deaf community in America*. Washington, DC: Gallaudet University Press.

van den Bogaerde, Beppie, and Anne Mills. 1994. Word order in language input to children: SLN or Dutch. In *Word-order issues in sign language: Working papers presented at a workshop held in Durham, 18–22 September 1991*, eds. Mary Brennan and Graham H. Turner, 133–57. Durham, UK: International Sign Linguistics Association.

Vermeerbergen, Myriam. 1996. ROOD KOOL TIEN PERSOON IN. Morfosyntactische Aspecten van Gebarentaal. PhD diss., Vrije Universiteit Brussel.

Vermeerbergen, Myriam. 2006. Past and current trends in sign language research. *Language & Communication* 26 (2): 168–92.

Volterra, Virginia, and Carol J. Erting. 1990. *From gesture to language in hearing and deaf children*. Berlin: Springer-Verlag.

Volterra, Virginia, Alessandro Laudanna, Serena Corazza, Elena Radutzky, and Francesco Natale. 1984. Italian Sign Language: The order of elements in the declarative sentence. In *Recent research on European Sign Language*, ed. Filip Loncke, Penny Boyes-Braem, and Yvan Lebrun, 19–46. Lisse, The Netherlands: Swets and Zeitlinger BV.

von Raffler-Engel, Walburga. 1980. Kinesics and paralinguistics: A neglected factor in second-language research and teaching. *Canadian Modern Language Review* 36 (2): 225–37.

Waibel, Alexander. 1988. *Prosody and speech recognition*. London: Pitman Publishing.

Wilbur, Ronnie B. 1985. Towards a theory of "syllable" in signed languages: Evidence from the numbers of Italian Sign Language. In *SLR' 83: International Symposium on Sign Language Research*, Rome, June 22–26, 1983, eds. William C. Stokoe and Virginia Volterra, 160–74. Silver Spring: Linstok Press.

Wilbur, Ronnie B. 1990. Why syllables? What the notion means for ASL research. In *Theoretical issues in sign language research*, eds. Susan Fisher and Patricia Siple, 81–108. Chicago: University of Chicago Press.

Wilbur, Ronnie B., and Susan B. Nolan. 1986. The duration of syllables in American Sign Language. *Language and Speech* 29:263–80.

Wojda, Piotr. 2010. Transmission of Polish sign systems. In *Sign languages*, ed. Diane Brentari, 131–148. Cambridge: Cambridge University Press.

BIBLIOGRAPHY

Woll, Bencie. 1991. Historical and comparative aspects of British Sign Language. In *Constructing deafness*, ed. Susan Gregory, 188–91. London: Continuum International Publishing Group.

Woll, Bencie. 2003. Modality, universality, and the similarities among sign language: An historical perspective. In *Cross-linguistic perspectives in sign language research*, eds. Anne Baker, Beppie van den Bogaerde, and Onno Crasborn, 17–27. Hamburg: Signum-Verlag.

Woll, Bencie, and Rachel Sutton-Spence. 2004. Sign language/Zeichensprache. In *Sociolinguistics: An international handbook of the science of language and society*. 2nd ed., ed. Ulrich Ammon, 677–83. Berlin: Walter de Gruyter.

Woodward, James. 1976. Signs of change: Historical variation in American Sign Language. *Sign Language Studies* 10:81–94.

Woodward, James. 1978. Historical bases of American Sign Language. In *Understanding language through sign language research*, ed. Patricia Siple, 333–48. New York: Academic Press.

Woodward, James. 1989. Some sociolinguistic aspects of French and American Sign Languages. In *Recent perspectives on American Sign Language*, eds. Harlan Lane and Francois Grosjean, 103–18. Mahwah, NJ: Lawrence Erlbaum.

Woodward, James. 2010. Some observations on research methodology in lexicostatistical studies of sign languages. In *Deaf around the world*, eds. Gaurav Mathur and Donna Jo Napoli, 50–71. Oxford: Oxford University Press.

Yau, Shun-chiu. 1990. Lexical branching in sign language. In *Theoretical issues in sign language research: Linguistics*, eds. Susan Fischer and Patricia Siple, 261–78. Chicago: University of Chicago Press.

Yau, Shun-chiu. 1992. *Creations gestuelle et debuts du langage: Creation de langues gestuelles chez des sourds isoles*. Paris: Editions Langages Croisés.

Yau, Shun-chiu. 2008. The role of visual space in sign language development. In *Space in languages of China*, ed. Dan Xu, 143–74. Berlin: Springer-Verlag.

Zeshan, Ulrike. 2000. *Sign language in Indo-Pakistan: A description of a signed language*. Amsterdam: John Benjamins.

Zeshan, Ulrike. 2003. "Classificatory" constructions in Indo-Pakistani Sign Language: Grammaticalization and lexicalization processes. In *Perspectives on classifier constructions in sign languages,* ed. Karen Emmorey, 113–42. Mahwah, NJ: Lawrence Erlbaum.

Zeshan, Ulrike. 2004a. Hand, head and face: Negative constructions in sign languages. *Linguistic Typology* 8 (1): 1–58.

Zeshan, Ulrike. 2004b. Interrogative constructions in signed languages: Cross-linguistic perspectives. *Language* 80 (1): 7–39.

Zeshan, Ulrike, ed. 2006. *Interrogative and negative constructions in sign languages*. Nijmegen, The Netherlands: Ishara Press.

INDEX

Figures and tables are indicated by f and t following page numbers. Italic page numbers indicate photographs.